Only a messenger

giving God glory through Jesus Christ

©2019

Be blessed, be blessed, and be very blessed!

Special thanks to:

My wife Lotte, son Grant, and daughter Paige.

Also

Linda & Kat

Hebrews 11:40 Since God had planned something better for us so that only together with us would they be made perfect.

Dear Friends,

The apostle Paul writes that we are disgraceful if all we have is hope in this life. That we are most pitiable among people. Well, I would like to suggest that we are just as disgraceful, pitiable really, if we have no hope at all. Make this year a year of joyful and expectant hope. The hope that God has something better for the world. Something better for us. Something better for our neighbor. Something better for our town. Something better for our state. Something better for our nation. See, God is moving. The spirit is being poured out. Revival is coming.

2 Corinthians 9:15 Thanks be to God for His indescribable gift!

Dear Friends,

What is God's indescribable gift? I know, it must be Jesus. Well, yes, Jesus is the one through whom this gift appeared, but the gift that is so indescribable is God's loving favor. It's the favor that increases one's wealth. The favor that makes us rich toward God and enlarges our harvest of righteousness. The favor that accompanies obedience to the Gospel and shows the world that God loves and cares for us. The favor that causes men and women's hearts to overflow with thanksgiving to God. It's God's loving favor, and Jesus said that this is the acceptable year.

1

2 Corinthians 4:16 Therefore we do not lose heart. Though outwardly we are wasting away, yet inwardly we are being renewed day by day.

Dear Friends,

This is a tremendous year in advancement for the Kingdom of God. I need not remind us that we are all part of this Kingdom, being adopted through faith in Jesus Christ. Sure, we all have troubles, we go through many struggles, but our souls magnify the Lord, for He has done great things. True, these bodies will not last. They are only temporary dwelling places for our eternal souls. Do not forget this, when our adoption is complete; we will have new eternal bodies. Therefore, we do not lose heart. We will not give up Kingdom advancement.

Mark 16:15 He said to them, "Go into all the world and preach the gospel to all creation."

Dear Friends,

We are going to reach out to all people with this winning message, the Gospel of Jesus Christ, for that is what the Lord has commanded us to do. We are reaching out to all people and winning the lost. Winning families, winning friends, winning co-workers, winning neighbors. We are winning, winning, winning! Also, we are baptizing, baptizing, baptizing. That's right; we are baptizing them in the Name of the Father, the Son, and the Holy Spirit. We are making disciples of all nations, and we are teaching them to obey the word of God. We will make the most of every opportunity to share this winning message with all boldness for this winning message is the power of God unto salvation.

1 Corinthians 15:34 Come back to your senses as you ought and stop sinning; for there are some who are ignorant of God—I say this to your shame.

Dear Friends,

It's time to get smart about eternal life and stop the crooked hellery. "Hellery" means wild and mischievous behavior. Sadly, many men and women have been misinformed about the true God and the life He has given us. All they know is the fake news. But we know the true news, the good news, the winning gospel of Jesus Christ. We know that there is eternal life in the Son. We need to tell them about Jesus today and show them that Jesus has changed our lives. Because, quite frankly, no one is promised tomorrow, at least not on this side of eternity.

Romans 16:19 Everyone has heard about your obedience, so I rejoice because of you; but I want you to be wise about what is good, and innocent about what is evil.

Dear Friends,

God wants us to get smart about doing the right thing and to be blameless about all corruption. That means we are going to have to make some hard decisions, and the other side is going to say that we are trying to push our own agenda. But we need to stand our ground. No compromise. God has promised that He will crush Satan. This I will say, that God will crush Satan under our feet. Now that's eternal security. So, let's stand together and continue to make God's kingdom great here on the earth.

/

2 Peter 1:11 And you will receive a rich welcome into the eternal kingdom of our Lord and Savior Jesus Christ.

Dear Friends,

It is so nice to receive a warm welcome, but quite frankly, I prefer a rich welcome. God warmly welcomes all men and women who believe in Jesus into His eternal kingdom, but there is an even richer, more glorious welcome for God's great and precious promises are given to those who believe in Jesus and participate in the divine nature. Well, many men and women are just fine with the idea of making it into glory, and I will say this, that better is one day there than a thousand elsewhere. But let's just make sure that we do not end up living a thousand elsewhere.

Ephesians 1:11 In him we were also chosen, having been predestined according to the plan of him who works out everything in conformity with the purpose of his will, . . .

Dear Friends,

We have been chosen by God to be conformed to the very image of His Son, Jesus. This is His plan, purpose, and will for our lives even before the creation. This means knowing Christ Jesus and participating in the divine nature. By knowing Christ Jesus, we are saved from this corrupt world and by participating in the divine nature, we reflect His glorious light. Now know this, that participation requires involvement. Do not ignore this call and hide that glorious light. Get smart and get involved. Remember this, we were created for good works in Christ.

Matthew 7:27 The rain came down, the streams rose, and the winds blew and beat against that house, and it fell with a great crash.

Dear Friends,

It is a foolish thing to hear the word of God but not to practice it. Think about it. It is just wisdom to practice safety guidelines when driving. When it is raining, we need to use the windshield wipers. When it is dark, we need to use the headlights, or when it is icy out, we need to use special caution. Quite frankly, if someone stops practicing the safety guidelines when operating the vehicle, they are likely to crash. But if they practice safety guidelines when operating the vehicle, they are able to make it home safely. Well, God wants to bring us safely home. Let's be wise and practice His guidelines, so we do not crash.

2 Peter 2:3 In their greed these teachers will exploit you with fabricated stories. Their condemnation has long been hanging over them, and their destruction has not been sleeping.

Dear Friends,

Let me mention and make everyone aware of the fake news that is in the church. They are not man's enemy as much as the enemy of the cross of Jesus Christ. They are the enemy of the Christian soul. That's right. These false teachers promise a better life but only take advantage of truth seekers like us. They teach made up stories that benefit themselves. Don't believe their lies. Don't listen to their arguments. Don't even give them the time of day. They are fake news. Just rebuke them with all authority for Jesus Christ has given us the authority, and the same Jesus gives us the Good News.

Proverbs 24:10 If you falter in a time of trouble, how small is your strength!

Dear Friends,

A believer is rewarded for great strength, and that strength is measured by endurance. It does not matter how hard a person can hit if that person just keeps on falling when they are hit back. Also, it is a very weak person who sits on the fence whenever calamity strikes. Now listen, because God has given us great power from on high, receive the Holy Spirit, and let the Spirit throw the punches. We just need to stand firm in God's mighty power. So, remember to trust in the Lord when faced with great opposition. His strength is great.

Matthew 10:14 If anyone will not welcome you or listen to your words, leave that home or town and shake the dust off your feet.

Dear Friends,

It is our responsibility to preach the message of Jesus Christ all over the world. Sadly, much of the world does not even want to hear this message. They don't want to hear about the blood that forgives us of our sins and cleanses us of all unrighteousness or the death that gives us life and the promise of something better. Do not lose heart or grow weary in well-doing. If we gave them the message, but they would not receive it well, quite frankly, we are not to give up the ministry. Remember this; it is the Lord who brings forth the harvests. We are only His messengers.

Galatians 6:14 May I never boast except in the cross of our Lord Jesus Christ, through which the world has been crucified to me, and I to the world.

Dear Friends,

There is a rule, that if we follow, we will gain the victory in all things. The rule is quite simple. If we believe in Jesus Christ and walk by faith in the Spirit, we will win. Sadly, the world will always try to cause us to walk in the flesh. But remember this, there is no final victory for those who walk in the flesh. Only overall loses. The flesh is always at war with the Spirit. Trying to awaken our sinful desires. But perfect peace and tender mercies belong to those who follow this rule. Oh, and by the way, if we believe in Jesus, we are the seed of Abraham, the Israel of God. Therefore, walk by faith in the Spirit.

/

2 Thessalonians 3:2 And pray that we may be delivered from wicked and evil people, for not everyone has faith.

Dear Friends,

If we want to see big wins for the Kingdom of God here on the earth, then we need to be the people of God here on the earth. That's important. Remember to pray for an accelerated sweep of the Gospel of Jesus Christ. Also, remember this, pray for God's anointed men and women because the world has become so very corrupt with unstable men and women who have no faith. Their wicked and evil intent is to obstruct this movement of the Gospel. But their efforts will end unsuccessfully because God is faithful. This I will say, He will govern His people forever.

James 1:21 Therefore, get rid of all moral filth and the evil that is so prevalent and humbly accept the word planted in you, which can save you.

Dear Friends,

Never build a house on loose gravel with no power to drive out life's dirt. Loose gravel may appear like the solid rock, but it has empty spaces in between the pieces of gravel. Well, life's dirt slips in between those empty spaces and causes the foundation to crack. When the foundation cracks, it's only a matter of time before the whole house comes crashing down. Remember this; if we want to build a firm foundation, we must humbly accept the word of God as the truth from God. Anything less than the truth might slip through the cracks. Then corruption will come in.

Hebrews 13:8 Jesus Christ is the same yesterday and today and forever.

Dear Friends,

Many Christians met Jesus yesterday when they first saw the light. They gladly suffered great ridicule and persecution for the Name of Jesus Christ. They proudly stood beside men and women that were laughed at for the same testimony. We all shared the same fire. We loved the good and hated evil. But somewhere along the line, we became lukewarm. Listen, God has not changed. It is our passion for Him that has changed. Remember this, that Jesus Christ is the expressed image of the Father and He is a Holy God forever. That will never change.

Proverbs 4:13 Hold on to instruction, do not let it go; guard it well, for it is your life.

Dear Friends,

Have you ever received a great gift, a really great gift and it came with a huge instruction manual? Well, maybe we read the basic operations but ignored any further instructions. Then years later someone might teach us what this really great gift can do. All that time was wasted and we missed so many great rewards. We received the gift, but life would have been so much greater if only we would have paid attention to the instructions. Well, salvation is a gift, but there is so much more that we can learn about this great salvation. Unless we take time and study the Bible, we may miss many of God's great rewards.

Hebrews 2:2 For since the message spoken through angels was binding, and every violation and disobedience received its just punishment,

Dear Friends,

The angels spoke the message of the law, and it was binding. Not one word of this law will pass away until all things are completed. But do not lose heart. For we know that He who began a good work is faithful to complete it, not only in us but in all of creation. Until the day of completion, we can be sure of this, that the blood of Jesus Christ has saved us, redeemed us, set us free from the penalty of the law. So, let's walk in the Spirit and continue to build God's standard of love, joy, peace, patience, kindness, goodness, faithfulness, gentleness, and self-control. For against such things, there is no law.

(

Proverbs 24:16 for though the righteous fall seven times, they rise again, but the wicked stumble when calamity strikes.

Dear Friends,

There was an honorable sea captain who owned a noble ship. One day the sea captain went on land, but he did not properly bind the ship to the dock. Sadly, the ship drifted away. But the captain did not just stand there and watch his ship sink into the ocean. No, the captain got back up. He swallowed his pride. He humbled himself and asked God for help. When one young fisherman offered him his little rowboat, the captain humbly accepted and paddled the rowboat thirty-five miles before he reached the ship. The captain suffered for a little while but in the end, his ship was recovered, and the captain's honor was restored.

1 John 1:5 This is the message we have heard from him and declare to you: God is light; in him there is no darkness at all.

Dear Friends,

Sin separates us from God. We are just lying to people if we claim to be in fellowship with God but go on sinning for in God there is no darkness. But if we keep in step with the Holy Spirit, we are continually washed in the blood of Jesus Christ. If we do sin, we are quick to repent, so we do not lose fellowship with God. When we lose fellowship with God, we lose fellowship with one another. So, let's live out the truth and walk in the light.

Psalm 16:11 You make known to me the path of life; you will fill me with joy in your presence, with eternal pleasures at your right hand.

Dear Friends,

With Jesus we have joy. So much joy. Great, great joy. It is joy unspeakable and full of glory. It's the joy of the Lord, and it is our strength. This great joy is down in our hearts, and it is here to stay. This joy is so great that we cannot even contain it. Really, we cannot contain it. It just burst out of our hearts, like a fountain, and it bubbles down in our souls. We are singing, laughing and dancing. That's right; we are dancing. Because of this great joy. Just singing, laughing, and dancing in the presence of the Lord.

2 Peter 3:17 Therefore, dear Friends, since you have been forewarned, be on your guard so that you may not be carried away by the error of the lawless and fall from your secure position.

Dear Friends,

When I say buckle up, what is the first thing that comes to mind? Maybe a seatbelt? Well, let's just take a look at the seatbelt. A seatbelt is for safety and security. As long as the person remains securely buckled in a seated position, they are safe from turbulence. It is when a person is unbuckled that they might get carried away. Listen now; we are coming into some turbulent times. Please remain seated in Jesus and buckled up. Also, make sure the seat is in an upright position. Listen to this; this is so important. I'm talking about being safe and secure, steadfast in Christ. Reconciled to God the Father through faith in God the Son. Growing in the grace and knowledge of the Lord Jesus Christ and maintaining that secure position. To Him be the glory forever and ever, amen!

/

Acts 15:19 It is my judgment, therefore, that we should not make it difficult for the Gentiles who are turning to God.

Dear Friends,

A little boy wanted to be like his father. His dad was overjoyed, and he decided that the boy should go to work with him the next day. On the next day, the father told the boy to wear a suit and tie to be like dad. So, the boy put on a suit and tie. At breakfast the father said, eat liver and onions to be like dad. The boy hated liver but ate it anyway. In the car, the dad said, "We drive in silence to be like dad." So, the boy never said a word. At work the father wanted to show the boy that he runs a tight ship, so he is very firm with all the employees. On the way home from work the boy tried to talk, but dad yelled, "I drive in silence son." After dinner mom asks, "Who wants dessert?" Father answered, "I skip dessert and watch the news." My point is this, dad was happy that his son wanted to be like him, but he failed to connect with the boy on a relational level. Now listen, salvation is not a list of dos and donts. It is a relationship. Sure, like all good relationships, it takes some work to maintain and keep it alive. Don't make it difficult. It's simply a loving relationship with God the Father through Jesus Christ.

1 Corinthians 10:13 No temptation has seized you except what is common to man. And God is faithful; he will not let you be tempted beyond what you can bear. But when you are tempted, he will also provide a way out so that you can stand up under it.

Dear Friends,

Some parents make their kids eat all their food for proper growth. Dad says things like, eat that food; it is good for strong muscles like Popeye. Sometimes the kids eat all their food, and it makes dad happy, and he gives them dessert. But sometimes they sit there and stare at the plate then dad might say take three more big bites, and then he would finish the rest. He is giving them a way to escape. They still had to eat three bites, but daddy finishes the rest. Listen, God has healthy growth in mind when He asks us to partake in Christ's sufferings. If we gladly partake of these sufferings, He will reward that. But if we sit there and stare at our plates, God helps us finish. Don't give in to temptation. Be strong. God is faithful.

James 1:17 Every good and perfect gift is from above, coming down from the Father of the heavenly lights, who does not change like shifting shadows.

Dear Friends,

We know that God is faithful and that He will provide a way out. Now, understand that the way out is not so that we can give in to that temptation. God will provide the way out so that we can stand up under that temptation. It's not a turning away from what we must endure, for there is no shadow of turning with God. It is His strength in our weakness to press on and take hold of that for which Christ Jesus took hold of us. That's every good and perfect gift.

Philippians 2:13 For it is God who works in you to will and to act in order to fulfill his good purpose.

Dear Friends,

God has compassion on our weaknesses, but He does not change His mind about what He wants us to accomplish. He's not going to sit there and say, "Well, they can't handle it, so I guess I'll have to go with plan B." There is no plan B with God because plan A never fails. God knows that there is too much on our plate. More than we can handle. More than we can digest. He desires that we stick with plan A and count it all Joy! So that we may be lacking in nothing then God may complete the good work He began. For God is faithful and He will complete it. This I will say, plan B, plan C, and plan D are not God's way out. God's way out is God's way through. His way is a breakthrough!

2 Timothy 4:18 The Lord will rescue me from every evil attack and will bring me safely to his heavenly kingdom. To him be glory for ever and ever. Amen.

Dear Friends,

Jesus tells us about two men. One a Pharisee and the other a tax collector. Both of them were in the temple praying. The Pharisee was full of pride and was confident that he was right with God. The tax collector humbled himself and cried out for mercy. It was the one whose heart was torn in two; it was the one who meant serious business with God as to say I'm not going to make it without God. It was the one who says save me, rescue me, show mercy. He was the one who went home justified, made right with God. See, it was that broken heart, that pain, that sorrow, that inner defeat that allowed the Holy Spirit to show the tax collector that he is lost on his own and in desperate need of God. Jesus is the Lord and Savior of all. Let's offer Him the cry of our heart today.

Matthew 10:34 "Do not suppose that I have come to bring peace to the earth. I did not come to bring peace, but a sword."

Dear Friends,

This scripture is very sobering. It cleans out the poisons of this world that pollute our minds and keep us from seeing clearly. What will distinguish the people of God from the rest of the world? Their money, power, or position? No! Maybe their heroic acts or supernatural abilities? No! How about their good looks or charming personality? No again! They are marked by a loving relationship with God through faith in Jesus Christ. Sadly, anyone who does not have that relationship is cut off from God. That relationship will separate God's people from the world. It is when we are divided from the world that we are united in Christ.

Matthew 25:13 Therefore keep watch, because you do not know the day or the hour.

Dear Friends,

One day the C.E.O and founder of the world's top firm and a foundation called his ten best and most faithful executives into his office. He told them he was going to be out of town for a little while and asked them to handle the company affairs while he was gone. Then he left. While the boss was gone, the demand grew, hours seemed long, and all the execs became tired. Only a few remained aware of company affairs, but the majority let matters go. Only a few received equal partnership and a rich inheritance when the boss returned. When the others tried to return, the boss said: "I do not recognize them."

Philippians 1:9 And this is my prayer: that your love may abound more and more in knowledge and depth of insight,

Dear Friends,

If we want to be pure and blameless when Jesus returns, then we must walk in the love of God, grow in His love, and clothe ourselves in His love. Noah found favor in the eyes of the Lord and God saved Noah and his family from destruction. What was it about Noah that God favored? His heart was not bent toward evil. He walked with God and God is love. The rest of mankind was only evil all the time. Jesus tells us, it will be like the days of Noah when He returns, and the love of most will grow cold. Let's not be like most. Let us be one of the few.

(

1 Peter 4:13 But rejoice in as much as you participate in the sufferings of Christ, so that you may be overjoyed when his glory is revealed.

Dear Friends,

A school teacher might say that the top ten percent of a student's grade will be based on participation. They don't care if the student likes the class or not, but they want to see the student in their seat and awake to get that "A." If the student is attentive, the teacher is pleased. When the test is returned, that attentive student may see a smiley face and well done written on their paper. God wants us in our assigned seats and a smile on our faces, especially when we don't like the lesson. The result is a great joy.

Are we winning?

1 John 1:6 If we claim to have fellowship with him and yet walk in the darkness, we lie and do not live out the truth.

Dear friends,

Just a word about the Holy Spirit whom God has placed in our hearts. The Holy Spirit is witness to the truth of Jesus Christ. If we hear a fake witness, then the Holy Spirit will speak to our hearts and lead us in all truth. But if we ignore the gentle voice of the Holy Spirit and walk in darkness, then the Holy Spirit becomes very silent in our hearts. The more that we silence the voice of the Holy Spirit, the harder it becomes to hear God. For God is Spirit. Sadly, we end up missing the promises of God. Let's take hold of the promises of God and allow the Holy Spirit to lead us.

Roman 3:24 And all are justified freely by his grace through the redemption that came by Christ Jesus.

Dear friends,

Know this; the angels long for the salvation that has been given us. The salvation in which we are freely justified. This salvation is through faith in the Lord Jesus Christ, and it is by grace. The angels have faith, but when they fell from grace, there was no return. They were instantly judged and forever condemned. When we fall from grace, and sadly we do fall, we are given more grace. It is grace upon grace because God so loved the world. This I will say, God, made us lower than the angels but redeemed us with His amazing grace.

Hebrews 12:7 Endure hardship as discipline; God is treating you as his children. For what children are not disciplined by their father?

Dear friends,

What happens when a child will not grow up and when a son or a daughter just continually feeds off the father's loving-kindness and goodness and takes daddy's unmerited favor lightly or for granted? Well, quite frankly, it's not good, one day the father's going to tell the child to leave the house, and the child will have to go off and learn life the hard way. It's not that daddy has abandoned the child. It's not that daddy will no longer help the child, but daddy wants the child to learn what is best so that the child becomes mature and lacking in nothing. Well listen, our heavenly Father wants the best for us. Only the best. So, step out in faith.

John 17:18 As you sent me into the world, I have sent them into the world.

Dear friends,

Under Christ's administration, we are making God's Kingdom great. We are standing up against the fake news and proclaiming the good news of Jesus Christ. We are winning the lost big, and God is glorified. We are seeping out the corrupt interest of the flesh and building God's standard which, by the way, is the fruit of the Holy Spirit. It's the movement, the movement of the Holy Spirit drawing the hearts of all men and women. So, let's seek first the kingdom of God, and His righteousness and God will do rest.

2 Chronicles 30:9 If you return to the Lord, then your fellow Israelites and your children will be shown compassion by their captors and will return to this land, for the Lord your God is gracious and compassionate. He will not turn his face from you if you return to him."

Dear friends,

Listen to this story about a father and his son. The son was playing with matches which alarmed his dad. The father yelled at him very loudly to correct the boy, but the boy mistook the father's correction as a coming punishment. The boy thought he better stay away until dad cools off. So, he spent the day hiding from his father. The father knew where the boy was but let him hide to learn what's best. When the boy came out, he said," I'm sorry dad, I'll never play with matches again." The father was so happy that the boy returned to him. He just looked at the boy and smiled, then he lovingly said, "It was just a warning son. If we play with matches, somebody gets burnt." My point is this, learn what's best and step out to embrace the Father's love.

Luke 21:38 Be always on the watch, and pray that you may be able to escape all that is about to happen, and that you may be able to stand before the Son of Man.

Dear friends,

A thief will come suddenly and unexpectedly when no one is watching. Then a thief will snatch the object and makes his escape. But an accomplished thief will also make a quick change. He will go from criminal to perfect citizen. The day of the Lord will come like a thief. God will remove the church, and they will escape. After they have escaped all that is coming on this earth, they will be changed in an instant and changed from corruptible to incorruptible. It sounds like the rapture of the church is the Lord's first order of business on that day.

Psalm 14:2 The Lord looks down from heaven on all mankind to see if there are any who understand, any who seek God.

Dear friends,

A master chef is renowned for their cooking. A film artist is greatly praised for their latest movie. A talented songwriter is celebrated for their number one hit. These creations are the splendor of a person's work. The grandeur of their accomplishments. To deny that person this glory is to disgrace their name. In the same way, the creation is the work of God's great hand. His signature is seen through what was made. To deny him glory is just foolishness. It is corruption. Worship the Lord. Does anyone understand?

Ephesians 1:9 He made known to us the mystery of his will according to his good pleasure, which he purposed in Christ,

Dear friends,

The mystery of Christ has been made known to us, and truthfully, we can expect every spiritual blessing. We know that it is God's good pleasure to bring Heaven and Earth together in unity under Christ. Once all things have been brought together in unity under Christ, then His Kingdom has come, and His will has been done here on the earth. Oh, and by the way, it is God's good pleasure to give us the Kingdom. So, let's pray together in Jesus Name for His Kingdom and agree together for every spiritual blessing.

∫

Matt 9:36 "When He saw the crowds, He had compassion on them, because they were harassed and helpless, like sheep without a shepherd.

Dear friends,

Remember the desperate days when we had no hope. The days when we had false hope like winning the lottery, drinking that bottle, or slipping in bed with that lover. Remember, God has not made us more than conquerors and destroyed the works of the devil in our lives so that we can come across as judgmental superheroes. No, not at all! He has called us to shine like stars. But that is not referring to the distant positioning of the light. It is referring to the mysterious quality of that light which although it is pure and piercing, it is gentle and inviting. So curious and distinctive that people are drawn to the peculiarity of that light. People imagine and invent ways to reach the source of that light. Let our light, so shine!

John 15:8 This is to my Father's glory, that you bear much fruit, showing yourselves to be my disciples.

Dear friends,

Jesus is the vine, and we are the branches. Unless we remain in Him, we cannot bear good fruit. I know that the word bear makes remaining in Jesus seem like a lot of work. I'm not going to lie. It is a little work but, is it a lot of work for a fruit tree to bear good fruit? Not if that tree is good. It is the nature of that tree when it is in season. Bearing good fruit should be in our nature both in and out of season. It is not a lot of work. It is remaining in Jesus. The world might call it a lot of work but let's call it our new redemptive nature.

Hebrews 6:12 We do not want you to become lazy, but to imitate those who through faith and patience inherit what has been promised.

Dear friends,

It is a disgrace to call ourselves a Christian but never grow in righteousness and to say we are clothed in the righteousness of Christ but never do the Father's will. That person is spiritually immature, dull in understanding and slow to move. They continually circle the same mountain trying to reach the top, but sadly, they may never see the promises of God for they will not step up in faith. But we are not like those who do nothing and call themselves holy. We are of those who follow Jesus and grow in righteousness.

Luke 20:25 He said to them, "Then give back to Caesar what is Caesar's, and to God what is God's."

Dear friends,

The elite of Jesus day sent spies to trap Jesus in His words. They tried to box Him in with a question about taxes owed to Caesar. They were hoping that His answer would warrant an arrest. But they could not box in the Son of God. His answer left them speechless. It put God's perspective on authority and made them think about the debt we owe God which, by the way, Jesus paid for in full. All authority is appointed by God, and the only debt that remains is to one another which is love. So, remain in Christ, walk in love, and leave the enemy speechless.

Mark 13:11 Whenever you are arrested and brought to trial, do not worry beforehand about what to say. Just say whatever is given you at the time, for it is not you speaking, but the Holy Spirit.

Dear friends,

We know this, the Spirit of God is mighty in power. Also, very important, the Holy Spirit is superior in wisdom. The religious elite tried to trap Jesus in His words. Looking for some statement, they could use against Him. Jesus knew in His Spirit that they were up to no good and His Spirit always gave Him great wisdom on how to answer. Christ Jesus has given up His Spirit, and the Father has given His Spirit to us. So, when we are on trial, the Spirit will give us a wise answer. Thank Jesus today for giving us His Spirit.

1 John 4:7 Dear friends, let us love one another, for love comes from God. Everyone who loves has been born of God and knows God.

Dear friends,

This is so important that we walk in love. That great big, massive, huge, love of God. Love that is so deep, so wide, so long, so high that it surpasses all knowledge. Its perfect love and it's fearless. Its tender love and it's tough. Its gentle love and it's strong. It suffers long, and it never fails. This I will say, God's love is the most excellent way. It never ends, never fails, and keeps on winning. God is love.

1 Corinthians 15:34 Come back to your senses as you ought, and stop sinning; for there are some who are ignorant of God—I say this to your shame.

Dear friends,

Sin will always try to desensitize our hearts toward the things of God. Things like His word, His righteousness, and His lost sheep. When we walk in the flesh, we become desensitized to the Holy Spirit and stop loving, stop caring, and stop doing the Father's will. Sadly, there are still people in this world who have not heard of this great salvation and they never will unless someone tells them. It is the Father's will that we tell them. Let us set aside the weight of sin and fix our eyes on Jesus, who always did the will of the Father.

Ephesians 4:7 But to each one of us grace was given according to the measure of Christ's gift.

Dear friends,

Let the love of Jesus be down in our hearts and take us from victory to victory. From triumph to triumph. From glory to glory. Let the unmerited favor of God be free on our lives and let the Holy Spirit influence our thoughts and regenerate our minds so that we have the mind of Christ. Let us strive for excellence and only be content to live godly lives through Christ Jesus. Let us reach perfection and let us do all of this according to what Christ has given us. It's winning grace, winning grace, winning grace.

1 John 4:11 Dear friends, since God so loved us, we also ought to love one another.

Dear friends,

When disaster or tragedy strikes the world and all around us, it is our distinct honor to show the world what God is made of. God is love. Nonstop, power packing, wonder-working relentless love. This love was expressed to us through Jesus Christ. We are to express this great love to one another through the power of the Holy Spirit. By doing this, it shows the world that we know God and that God is in us. No one has ever seen God, but God's love is made complete in us. Gratefully, we are like Jesus in this world. Be like Jesus and walk in love.

Romans 6:11 In the same way, count yourselves dead to sin but alive to God in Christ Jesus.

Dear friends,

What does it mean when someone says consider me dead? It means that they will no longer give place to the other person. The other person might continually beg them to return, but when someone is serious, they will make no room for that person in their life. Similarly, we need to be serious about righteousness and consider ourselves dead to sin. Listen, sin will always try to tempt us to return to that sin continually. But remember this, Jesus set us free from sin, and it is no longer our master.

Philemon 1:6 I pray that your partnership with us in the faith may be effective in deepening your understanding of every good thing we share for the sake of Christ.

Dear friends,

How good and pleasant it is when believers partner together in the faith. When brothers and sisters fellowship in Jesus Name and encourage one another with Christ's love. When the rain of the Spirit is poured out like fresh oil on our heads. I'm talking about the rain of the Holy Spirit just falling on our heads. That's when the hidden things of God are made know, and the Holy Spirit will deepen our understanding to receive all of Christ's benefits. Benefits that every believer is welcome to enjoy. Let's partner together, so that our faith may be made effective.

James 4:15 Instead, you ought to say, "If it is the Lord's will, we will live and do this or that."

Dear friends,

It is prided to think we can win life without doing the will of the Father. That's not to say that we won't see the goodness of the Lord here on the Earth. However, if we want to see God's goodness in times of trouble, we better be about His business. Do not boast about plans for the future for the outcome of life is really in the hands of the Lord. People say, tomorrow we will go here or tomorrow we will do this. Only God knows tomorrow. We need to seek Jesus if we want to win tomorrow and follow Jesus if we want to win life.

1 Corinthians 15:2 By this gospel you are saved, if you hold firmly to the word I preached to you. Otherwise, you have believed in vain

Dear friends,

The faith that brings salvation comes by hearing the gospel message and believing what we have heard. Faith acts on what it believes. Faith not only acts on what it believes but faith holds firm to that belief. The book of the Bible that records the faith of the early church is called the book of Acts. The book of Acts records men and women who acted in faith upon the gospel of Jesus Christ and the Holy Spirit empowered them to do the will of the Father. Know this, their belief was not in vain for Jesus will recognize them forever.

James 2:26 As the body without the spirit is dead, so faith without deeds is dead.

Dear friends,

We know that without faith it is impossible to please God. For whoever comes to God must, first of all, believe that He exists, and second of all, that He is a rewarder of those who truly seek Him. Many people believe in God, but their faith is superficial. It lacks any real substance and is without effect. It doubts the faithfulness of God and that God will answer their prayers. It is unsure of what it hoped for and uncertain of what it prayed. It will not even act on the things it does not see. Let's not even call it faith. Let's call it fake faith.

Matthew 7:21 "Not everyone who says to me, 'Lord, Lord,' will enter the kingdom of heaven, but only the one who does the will of my Father who is in heaven.

Dear friends,

There was a soldier who was great in battle. He would fight for his people. He would fight for truth and justice. Until one day, he was brutally attacked and badly wounded. The soldier gave up the fight, he lost hope and sadly, he was taken captive by the enemy. One day, he was rescued and returned home. Many people recognized him, and they called him a great war hero, but other people would not welcome him home because he lost hope. Jesus tells us that He will only recognize those who do the will of His Father in heaven. They do not give up the fight. They do not lose hope. They will be welcomed home.

James 5:18 Again he prayed, and the heavens gave rain and the earth produced its crops.

Dear friends,

Elijah knew the power of prayer. He prayed again and again. Elijah prayed seven times before he saw a little cloud. That little cloud was all the evidence that Elijah needed to declare that God was going to make it rain. This evidence is all around us, and it is overwhelming. God is going to make it rain in these last days. Times of refreshing are coming. Days of revival. The land will be healed. The earth will produce its crop and souls will be harvested. I do believe so. It's a fervent prayer.

2 Peter 2:9 If this is so, then the Lord knows how to rescue the godly from trials and to hold the unrighteous for punishment on the day of judgment.

Dear friends,

A time of trial is coming on this whole world to test the inhabitants of this earth. A time in which God's wrath will be poured out on corrupt individuals that despise authority. This happened before in the days of Noah and these days will be even worse. No one wants to be a part of these days but thanks to God we have a way out. That way out is to live a godly life through faith in Christ Jesus, to be awake, and to keep our lamps burning. The Lord knows how to rescue us, and He has promised to do so. To Him be the glory forever and ever, Amen.

James 5:12 Above all, my brothers and sisters, do not swear – not by heaven or by earth or by anything else. All you need to say is a simple 'Yes' or 'No'. Otherwise, you will be condemned.

Dear friends,

When a person makes a bad deal, they need to be able to cut their losses and return to God quickly. It's getting out of the bad deal and into our great God. But when a person makes a bad deal, and they swear on it, they become bound to an agreement. If they break that agreement, their hearts will be condemned. But remember, there is no condemnation for those who are in Christ Jesus because they walk by the Spirit. Let no one condemn those whom God has justified. Keep it simple. Walk in the Spirit. Be honest, be true, and be uncorrupt.

Hebrews 2:18 Because he himself suffered when he was tempted, he is able to help those who are being tempted.

Dear friends,

When we are tempted with more than we can bear, we begin to think we are the only ones who have to go through this thing. No one else and there is no way out. This is just not true. It is a lie from the devil to rob us of the grace of God in our lives. Many people are tempted in this way. Jesus was tempted in this way. He walked in our shoes. He knows our battles. He has been there and overcame that. So, we too can overcome that. Let's give thanks to Jesus who always leads us forward in triumph.

Luke 13:34 Jerusalem, Jerusalem, you who kill the prophets and stone those sent to you, how often I have longed to gather your children together, as a hen gathers her chicks under her wings, and you were not willing.

Dear friends,

It is whosoever will. The blood of Jesus cries out mercy over all men and women, "Father forgive them for they know not what they do." Jesus longs for us and is crying out," Come to me, and I will give you rest." Jesus wants to gather us in His loving arms and keep us from all that is coming on this earth. Sadly, many men and women are not willing, and they will perish. Do not reject the Son of God like Jerusalem did. They will not see Him again until they willingly receive Him. Let us open our hearts and invite Jesus in.

Yes, I do believe we are winning. Keep on winning!

*Philippians 3:18 For, as I have often told you before
and now tell you again even with tears, many live as
enemies of the cross of Christ.*

Dear friends,

There are many beautiful but lost people in the
world. Many of them have heard the gospel, but still,
they choose to ignore it. They are slaves to their sin.
Sadly, their end is destruction. A destiny that we all
once shared but Jesus saved us, and Jesus made us
citizens of His Kingdom. That's right, and Jesus
changed us. He took away all our sin. So, let's follow
Jesus' example and show compassion to the lost. That
means we should weep over the lost as Jesus wept
over the city of Jerusalem. How He longed to gather
them in His arms, but they were not willing. Cry out
for a lost loved one today.

1 Timothy 1:19 Holding on to faith and a good conscience, which some have rejected and so have suffered shipwreck with regard to the faith.

Dear friends,

Why does a skipper bind his ship to the dock when he is on the land? Because in good conscience he knows the ship must be properly grounded or it may drift away. If it drifts away, it may go shipwreck. So, the skipper will do everything he can to make sure that the ship is not moved. Now Listen, it is so important that we hold on to hope we have in Jesus as an anchor for our souls. That we bind the word of God to our hearts so that we are not moved. Let's get well grounded in the word of God so that our faith does not go shipwreck.

Romans 8:19 For the creation waits in eager expectation for the children of God to be revealed.

Dear friends,

There is a day coming when God will reveal to the whole creation who are His sons and daughters. Sadly, until that day comes, the whole creation will wait for this revealing. But we don't need this revealing to know we are God's sons and daughters. Let's not forget the daughter's, for they are very important to God too. God told the creation it was not good without the women. Yes, we know we are God's children because His Spirit bears witness with our spirits that we are children of God. So, we eagerly wait for Jesus to be revealed.

2 Corinthians 7:10 Godly sorrow brings repentance that leads to salvation and leaves no regret, but worldly sorrow brings death.

Dear friends,

Don't cry over spilled milk. I know it sounds so cliché, but that is a result of godly sorrow. Godly sorrow brings repentance. For our hearts are broken as we confess our sinfulness to a holy God. That is the result of Godly sorrow that brings repentance, and it leads to salvation. There is no place for worldly sorrow. The blood of Jesus has washed away all our sins and made us clean. Do not wallow in past sins like a pig wallowing in the mud. That is what the devil wants us to do. Resist the devil, and he will flee. Follow Jesus and don't cry over spilled milk.

1 John 2:28 And now, dear children, continue in him, so that when he appears, we may be confident and unashamed before him at his coming.

Dear friends,

Are we winning? I think we are winning. Because I have read to the end of the book and God's people are victorious. That's us Church. The details are a bit messy, and quite frankly, there are many different opinions on the order of events. But one thing is clear when Christ Jesus appears; we will appear with Him in Glory. Does that sound like a win? That sounds like a big win. So, let's make Christ Jesus our lives and be guided by His Holy Spirit. Don't miss this great salvation. When the devil tries to stop us, we will remind the devil who is winning.

Titus 3:6 Whom he poured out on us generously through Jesus Christ our Savior,

Dear friends,

What happens when an event is rained out? Well, it becomes interrupted and rescheduled. How long depends on the heaviness of the rain. It could be pushed back for one hour, or the event could be moved to a whole other day. If it keeps on raining on the rescheduled day, then things get pushed back even farther. Well, the rain of the Spirit is falling, and it is only going to intensify in these last days. How long it lasts may depend on our response to this outpouring. I can say this: if we respond through faith in Jesus Christ, the Father is quite lavish.

/

Mark 13:36 If he comes suddenly, do not let him find you sleeping.

Dear friends,

Does anything come more suddenly than a bolt of lightning? It lights up the whole sky. When lightning strikes in the east people can see it in the west. People run to their windows to see shots of electricity going through the air. They become caught up watching and waiting for each flash of light. Well, when Jesus returns it will be like lightning in the sky and those who are awake will be caught up in a flash to meet the Lord in the sky. Listen Church, now is not the time to fall asleep. Jesus is coming. It's time to get right and get caught up.

2 Corinthians 4:7 But we have this treasure in jars of clay to show that this all-surpassing power is from God and not from us.

Dear friends,

Contained in our human bodies are a treasure chest filled with Holy Spirit power, bearing witness to the gospel of Jesus Christ. It is God's awesome power being displayed by signs, wonders, various miracles, and spiritual gifts that advance His Kingdom. The enemy is terrified by this. So, the enemy will cause us trouble to stop Kingdom advancement. But it's not going to work. We will take heart and not give up. We will share the wealth and testify to this great salvation, and it is a great salvation. Displaying God's glory in the face of Jesus Christ.

John 18:21 Why question me? Ask those who heard me. Surely they know what I said."

Dear friends,

The world has always questioned Jesus and His words. They do not want to believe what He said. He said that He is the way, the truth, and the life. That no one goes to the Father except for through Him. Whoever believes in Jesus, though they were dead, yet they will live. Many, many men and women who also heard Jesus bear witness to this great salvation. God is still using men and women in the Church to testify of this great salvation, accompanied by the power of the Holy Spirit. Let anyone who has ears to hear, get strong and be a witness.

2 Thessalonians 1:8 He will punish those who do not know God and do not obey the gospel of our Lord Jesus.

Dear friends,

The enemy is spreading lies, throwing God's people into confusion. Reporting on the fake news. Trying to make God's people doubt the message that they first heard and were saved. The message that Jesus Christ is the Son of God. He died for our sins. He was buried, resurrected, ascended on high, That He is coming back for us. They make light of God's word and say where is this coming that He promised? But God is not mocked. He is patient with all people giving them time to repent. They will pay for their lies. I'm not saying who they are, but the devil and everyone that he deceives will pay, Trust and obey the true Gospel of Jesus Christ.

Jeremiah 26:13 Now reform your ways and your actions and obey the Lord your God. Then the Lord will relent and not bring the disaster he has pronounced against you.

Dear friends,

Now God has done something really incredible with the debt that we owed Him. He has canceled it for everyone that believes in Jesus. It's the forgiveness of sins and eternal life. Now, that is a big win. A really big win. This, I will say, it is so nice to receive God's amazing grace. Now, God expects us to reform our ways and actions and obey Him through faith in Jesus Christ. God promises that He will reward that. Believe God when He tells us that it will be so nice to receive all of God's promises when Jesus Christ appears. So, let's get right and reform our ways!

1 John 4:1 Dear friends, do not believe every spirit, but test the spirits to see whether they are from God, because many false prophets have gone out into the world.

Dear friends,

There are a real evil and deceptive spirit in the world today. It is the antichrist spirit, and many, many people are controlled of them. They make a deliberate stand against the Name of Jesus and deny the incarnation. They are wolves in sheep's clothing, Ferocious wolves tickling the itching ears of men and women. Well, many of these men and women once knew God and loved Jesus. They may have even worked for His Kingdom but not anymore. They have fallen away and joined the deep apostate. Do not be deceived.

James 1:22 Do not merely listen to the word, and so deceive yourselves. Do what it says.

Dear friends,

Last time we talked about the deep apostate, which, by the way, is run by lawless spirits of antichrist. Many, many people have been deceived by these lawless spirits. But sadly, we have the power to deceive ourselves into lawlessness. See, God has given to each one of us free will. This means that we can choose how we respond to the news we hear. If we hear the Good news and we make the bad news, well then, we call that fake news. But if we listen carefully to the word of God and are obedient to do what God said. This much I will say, that person is living truth, and they will be blessed.

*Galatians 4:9 But now that you know God—or rather
are known by God—how is it that you are turning back
to those weak and miserable forces? Do you wish to be
enslaved by them all over again?*

Dear friends,

Remember the women caught in adultery.
Well, the crowd wanted to stone the women, but
Jesus said to the crowd "Let he who is without sin
throw the first stone." Well, because they were all
guilty of sin, no one could throw the first stone. See,
Jesus had saved the women, and He set her free. She
was free indeed. Now, Jesus said to the woman,
"neither do I condemn you. Go and sin no more," Now
listen to this, because this is very important. Jesus told
the woman to go and sin no more because to continue
in that sin would only compromise her freedom. Let's
not compromise our freedom. Can we do that?

2 Corinthians 4:10 We always carry around in our body the death of Jesus, so that the life of Jesus may also be revealed in our body.

Dear friends,

Who remembers the old Timex commercial? Takes a licking but keeps on ticking. Well, in a similar way our bodies take a licking. They are persecuted, hard pressed, and perplexed. They are struck down but not destroyed. At times we want to give up, but these troubles are working out a far greater weight of eternal glory. It's time to get tough and seek first. Get smart, seek His righteousness also. For though our bodies are wasting away, our souls are being refreshed, renewed, transformed day by day. Our bodies may take a licking, but our souls will keep on ticking.

Luke 6:46 "Why do you call me, 'Lord, Lord,' and do not do what I say?

Dear friends,

Jesus compares a strong builder to a weak builder. A wise builder to a foolish one. Well, may I remind everyone that we have all been called to build the Kingdom of God here on the earth. Not only have we been called to build God's Kingdom here on the earth, but we have been called to make His Kingdom great. Now, if we are going to make a great Kingdom, then it needs to be a strong Kingdom. A Kingdom that will not be shaken. Built on a firm foundation. Based on the pattern that God has given to us. Now, Jesus is that firm foundation and the word of God is that pattern. Get smart and make His Kingdom great.

Romans 8:22 We know that the whole creation has been groaning as in the pains of childbirth right up to the present time.

Dear friends,

We should not be groaning about these present-day troubles Sure we will all have troubles in this world, but we are not longing to be set free like the rest of creation. See, Jesus has already set us free, and we are free indeed. Therefore, we may groan inwardly because the Spirit of God is teaching us how to pray, but outwardly, we rejoice. Because these troubles are light and momentary. They do not last. Be filled with the Holy Spirit and be of good cheer. Jesus has overcome this world, and He has made us more than conquerors.

Hebrews 3:12 See to it, brothers and sisters, that none of you has a sinful, unbelieving heart that turns away from the living God.

Dear friends,

Do not think that God will reward us if we hold on to sin. If someone is aware of sin in their life but holds on to it, it may cause them to miss God's promise. It is disobedience and unbelief toward God. Well, remember, John 3:16, whoever believes in Him will inherit. So do not let our hearts become disobedient or unbelieving and ignore this great salvation. We must pay the most careful attention to what we hear. Listen for the voice of the Holy Spirit. The Holy Spirit will lead us in all truth. Remember, God will reward that. So, let's get smart and seek first?

Hebrews 2:3 How shall we escape if we ignore so great a salvation? This salvation, which was first announced by the Lord, was confirmed to us by those who heard him.

Dear friends,

What can we expect when we ignore so great a salvation? Well, quite frankly, it is disgraceful. We can expect to receive nothing of eternal value. To have no real and lasting hope in this life and to receive no grace in the life to come. But what can we expect when we are attentive to this great salvation? Well, we can expect good things. We can expect to have real and lasting hope in this life. To see the goodness of the Lord here on the earth. We can expect to escape fire and judgment, fire and judgment. We can expect to receive God's glorifying grace when He appears. Oh, and by the way, we can expect eternal life. Does that sound ok?

Philippians 2:12 ...continue to work out your salvation with fear and trembling,

Dear friends,

We need to work out our salvation daily with fear and trembling. Fear and trembling. Not with a fear that our sin is too great for God to forgive. But with trembling that our sinfulness has offended God and therefore, we need His forgiveness. We all need God's forgiveness daily. That is why we must work out our salvation every day. With fear and trembling. For it is a fearful thing to fall into the hands of an angry God. So, let's remain in His loving favor, in His graces, and be quick to repent. God is faithful to forgive us of all our sins and He will remember them no more.

Romans 8:18 I consider that our present sufferings are not worth comparing with the glory that will be revealed in us.

Dear friends,

There is no doubt that in this world we will have troubles, we can be sure of this, but we need to see these troubles as light and momentary. Light and momentary. For they will not last, like a bad joke. "Why did the chicken cross the road? To get to the other side." It's a bad joke. Not very funny. It's foolish, and the humor does not last very long. Well, in a similar way our troubles will not last very long, and they are ridiculously trivial in comparison to the glory that awaits us. I'm not trying to minimize anyone's pain, but I am saying that we all need to remember that Jesus went to prepares a place for us.

Hebrews 7:25 Therefore he is able to save completely those who come to God through him, because he always lives to intercede for them.

Dear friends,

What does it mean when someone says, "I will destroy them"? Well, it means they will disgrace their name and end their legacy. Well, when the Son of God came to this earth, He left quite a legacy. His legacy brought good news, healing, deliverance, and salvation to all who believe. From the time that Jesus was a baby, the devil tried to destroy His legacy. But Jesus continued to grow in favor with God and men. Then the devil thought he would destroy Jesus on the cross. But Jesus' life was indestructible. Jesus defeated death and lives forever. Celebrate that victory this Easter.

Matthew 6:10 Your kingdom come,

Your will be done,

on earth as it is in heaven.

Dear friends,

Jesus left quite a legacy on this earth and not so we would bury it but so that we might carry it. Jesus lived a legacy of complete obedience to the Father. So, when we are obedient to the Father through faith in Christ Jesus, we continue this legacy. This means being humble and submitting to God's will. That was how Jesus taught us to pray. Thy Kingdom come, thy will be done. On earth, as it is in Heaven. Jesus emptied himself and was obedient even unto the point of death. But God raised Him on the third day. That's right, giving Him the highest Name. So, go out, in the Name of Jesus, and continue His legacy.

John 18:11 So Jesus said to Peter, "Put your sword into the sheath. Shall I not drink the cup which My Father has given Me?"

Dear friends,

God has given each one of us a cup that we must bear, and it is a cup of suffering. I'm not saying that God has created the world's suffering, but God will use the world's suffering to bring us into His glory. It is this fallen world that has created our suffering. God only has good things for each of us, so we proudly bear with the world's suffering until we reach perfection. Because when perfection comes, the imperfect will pass away. Now I will say this; if we can focus on Jesus and have faith in Him, then we will become aware of the glory that is laid up for us. Then we will gladly endure these light and momentary troubles.

1 Peter 2:11 Dear friends, I urge you, as foreigners and exiles, to abstain from sinful desires, which wage war against your soul.

Dear friends,

Peter stresses this point. It is like he's waving a red flag on this one. Saying listen up. We need to do what is right at all cost. It's a battle out there for our souls. The ruler of this world wants to destroy our souls, and if we step over to his side, then we put our souls in harm's way. But if we remember that we are not of this world, that we are strangers to this world's system, and this world hates us. Then we will steer clear of worldly passions, we will proceed with caution, and ultimately, God will be glorified.

Titus 2:6 Similarly, encourage the young men to be self-controlled.

Dear friends,

If we are going to seep out that massive seed of corruption, we call the flesh, then we need to have some self-control. It's not a matter of self being controlled by self. Although that is part of it. Now listen, because this is very important. It is self being controlled by the Holy Spirit. Giving the Holy Spirit complete control of our lives, so we do not fall into the error of lawlessness. We will live disciplined lives, and we will not lose our stability. We will obey God's command to walk in love, being filled with the Holy Spirit. It's freedom in Christ, freedom in Christ.

Luke 9:62 Jesus replied, "No one who puts a hand to the plow and looks back is fit for service in the kingdom of God."

Dear friends,

Anyone who wants to work for God must be willing to completely separate themselves from the world for the work of the Kingdom. It is separate themselves from the world for the work of God. The world is corrupt and the things of the world are corrupt. If anyone loves the world, the love of the Father is not in them. It is disgraceful. But if we will separate ourselves from this world and do not look back. This I will say, we will shine with the light of the gospel and the glory of Jesus Christ. When people see our good works, they will give glory to God.

John 8:11 "Then neither do I condemn you," Jesus declared. "Go now and leave your life of sin."

Dear friends,

It is time to get the sin out. It is time to drain the swamp. I'm talking about that wicked, evil seed of corruption that we call the flesh. It's disastrous, and quite frankly, it's disgraceful to even talk about the things that people do in the flesh. The truth is that we are all guilty of it. We have all become fleshly. But Jesus does not condemn us before the Father. There is no condemnation for those who are in Christ Jesus. Only forgiveness of sins and reconciliation with God. But we need to be in Christ Jesus. This, I will say, the result is eternal life.

Romans 13:14 Rather, clothe yourselves with the Lord Jesus Christ, and do not think about how to gratify the desires of the flesh.

Dear friends,

We have to build that standard. This is our reasonable act of service to God who has set us free from the power of corrupt interests. The flesh is corrupt, and its interests are no good. The flesh is very bad. Quite frankly, the flesh will profit us nothing. We will make no provision for the flesh. Don't even think about it or how to gratify it. So important, what we were powerless to do God did by sending His Son in the flesh, but His flesh knew no corruption. Therefore, we too can have power over the flesh by walking in the Spirit. For the Spirit gives life in Christ.

2 Peter 1:12 So I will always remind you of these things, even though you know them and are firmly established in the truth you now have.

Dear friends,

When the enemy comes at us like a flood, we will do what? That's right; I heard somebody say it. We will build that standard. Don't even think about it. We have no excuse. We have to build that standard, and the enemy will shudder. Because this is going to be a great standard. It will consist of love, joy, peace, patience, kindness, goodness, faithfulness, gentleness, and very important, self-control. That's right, and it is our faith in Jesus Christ and walking in His Holy Spirit that makes this standard a mighty fortress. Quite frankly, a mighty fortress is our God.

1 Thessalonians 5:24 The one who calls you is faithful, and he will do it.

Dear friends,

Building God's standard can be a real struggle. The work, and it does take work, can be very difficult and painful at times. This means that we are going to have to discipline ourselves if we want to see real progress. Our enemy, the devil, is always trying to stop our progress. Sometimes it seems like the progress is very great and other times it seems like the progress has completely stopped. But know this, that God is working out our glory even when it seems like no progress is being made at all. Now, this is so important, never give up. Just continue working and trust the Lord that the standard will be built.

Let us boast in the Lord.
Still winning!

Hebrews 12:9 Moreover, we have all had human fathers who disciplined us and we respected them for it. How much more should we submit to the Father of spirits and live.

Dear friends,

Plain and simple. Plain and simple. We need to learn how to do the will of the Father even when it seems like a struggle. We need to learn how to submit to the Father's authority with great joy and eager expectation. Because quite frankly, Daddy knows how to win the lost and he desires that the lost be won. Listen, God has winning plans for each of us. Trust in Him and follow His plan; all things will work out heavenly. Even things that seem disastrous. Look at the cross. How God turned what appeared to be a great disaster into this great salvation.

Isaiah 26:3 You will keep in perfect peace

those whose minds are steadfast,

because they trust in you.

Dear friends,

I want everyone to experience true and lasting peace, peace, wonderful peace. The peace of God. the peace that passes all understanding. That's right; this peace is so great that we cannot even understand it. I want it to flow, flow, flow like a river in our souls. So, let me tell everyone where they can find this perfect peace. It is only in Christ Jesus. Yes, enter into a loving, faith-based, trusting relationship with Jesus. Let the peace of Christ rule in our hearts and let the Holy Spirit govern our minds and let the peace of God, let it reign.

1 Corinthians 6:14 By his power God raised the Lord from the dead, and he will raise us also.

Dear friends,

It is the power that raised Jesus from the dead. It is the power that Jesus gave us, so we to could overcome this world. It is the power that Jesus told His disciples to wait for in the upper room. It is the power that Jesus tells us to pray for, so that we may be found worthy to escape. It is the power that keeps our lamps burning even when we fall asleep. It is the power of the Holy Spirit. This power overflows from the riches of God. Be rich toward God and receive more of God's dynamite power.

Luke 13:43 Jesus answered him, "Truly I tell you, today you will be with me in paradise."

Dear friends,

Remember the two criminals that hung on the crosses next to Jesus? Well, one overlooked his guilt; the other confessed it. One held on to his pride; the other humbled himself. One mock Jesus as the Christ, the other said, remember me, Lord, when you enter into your Kingdom. One perished in his sin, and the other entered into eternal life. My point is this, whatever sin is in someone's life is never too big for God to forgive. Christ died for the sinner. Cry out to Jesus. He remembers us, and He forgives our sins.

Psalm 27:13 I remain confident of this: I will see the goodness of the Lord in the land of the living.

Dear friends,

It is faith in Jesus Christ and obeying God's command to walk in love that completes the love of God in us. Since God's love is being made complete in each of us, let us remain confident God has good things in store for us, things that will prosper us and not harm us. Things that will give us hope for the future. As long as we remain confident in Jesus Christ, we have nothing to fear. His love makes us fearless. Know this; God's perfect love will drive out every fear. Now, because of Jesus we can be confident that God hears our prayers, God forgives our sins, and God will heal our land.

Matthew 5:12 Rejoice and be glad, because great is your reward in heaven, for in the same way they persecuted the prophets who were before you.

Dear friends,

We got to be bold, we got to be strong, and we got to take pride in the Name of Jesus. Be glad that we bear His Name. That the Spirit of God and glory rest upon us. Rejoice when we are insulted. Celebrate when we are persecuted. Shout with joy when someone spreads fake news about us for the Name of Jesus Christ. Just shake the dust off those shoes and keep on serving the Lord with gladness. For we are blessed and great is our reward in heaven.

Matthew 25:29 For whoever has will be given more, and they will have an abundance. Whoever does not have, even what they have will be taken from them.

Dear friends,

If we, the people of God, want to know His mighty power. By the way, God is all powerful. If we want to share in His glorious riches. So that everyone knows, God is exceedingly rich. Then we must work hard and exercise the good gifts that God has given to each one of us. We cannot settle for mediocrity. It is wickedness to bury the investment that God has made in our lives, and it is laziness that will keep us, yes, laziness will keep us, from a profitable return on that investment. Know this, everyone, yes everyone, that shows a profitable return will be richly rewarded.

Romans 5:6 You see, at just the right time, when we were still powerless, Christ died for the ungodly.

Dear friends,

Today let's talk about a really great salvation, and it is a great salvation. The first man that God ever created sinned against God. As a result, sin entered the world. Sin reigned, and sin reigned for thousands and thousands of years. But when the time was right, God sent His Son in the image of sinful man to redeem mankind. Know this, because of that one man's disobedience all mankind died. Both men and women. But because of Jesus Christ's righteousness, we can now inherit eternal life. Now this, I will say, that whoever believes in Jesus will never die.

Romans 8:17 Now if we are children, then we are heirs—heirs of God and co-heirs with Christ, if indeed we share in his sufferings in order that we may also share in his glory.

Dear friends,

We must be proud of our glorious heritage. An inheritance to everlasting life through messiah's bloodline. This is the bloodline of Jesus Christ, and it flows from the cross. It cleanses us from all our sins and makes us children of God. And as children of God, we are co-heirs with Christ Jesus. We will share in His glory as long as we do not give up our birthright. Do not be like Esau who gave up his birthright for a single meal. Hold on to this birthright with patient endurance. The promised inheritance is very near.

\

2 Thessalonians 3:6 Keep away from every believer who is idle and disruptive and does not live according to the teaching you received from us.

Dear friends,

Did you know that there are disruptors in the church? Men and women who are believers, yet they are quick to quarrel and raise controversies. Sure, we all have questions, but these disruptors are not seeking answers. They seek to disrupt the unity within Christ's administration. Once the unity is disrupted the whole administration begins to crumble. Know this, a kingdom divided against itself cannot stand. Sadly, that is what these disruptors do. They cause division. But if we know God's word and we are careful to obey it, then no disruption will divide us. We will all remain as one in the Spirit of unity.

Romans 12:2 Do not conform to the pattern of this world, but be transformed by the renewing of your mind. Then you will be able to test and approve what God's will is—his good, pleasing and perfect will.

Dear friends,

The reworking of our minds is so important in the renewal process. It means the difference between being troubled people to becoming a winning people. Not that we won't have trouble but that we will know in all these things that we are more than conquerors. It's time that we realized that we are working on a broke system. We will change our ways and renew our minds with the word of God. Becoming more like Christ. Then we will know what God's good, pleasing, and perfect will is. Good things will happen, and we will always be winning people.

Luke 18:27 Jesus replied, "What is impossible with man is possible with God."

Dear friends,

Faith has proven time and time again that there is no power more awesome, more unstoppable, than the hand of almighty God. Since the creation of this world, no power has ever been greater. To the Revelation of Jesus Christ, God's authority cannot be matched. But people don't want to believe the facts. They would much rather believe the fake news. I'm never going to get any better. This marriage is never going to work. I'm never going to break free from this dept. This world has a real problem believing God. But if we will earnestly seek the Lord our God, believe God when He says, nothing, nothing, nothing is impossible.

Mark 9:23 "'If you can'?" said Jesus. "Everything is possible for one who believes."

Dear friends,

All power and authority have been given to us through Jesus Christ. Truly, through Christ Jesus, we really do have great power and authority. Ask, and it will be given, seek and we will find, knock and the door will be opened. Anything we ask in Jesus Name will be given to us. Why? Because our hearts aim to please God and we do what He says. Now believe this; nothing is impossible with God!

2 Corinthians 10:3 For though we live in the world, we do not wage war as the world does.

Dear friends,

It is so important that we are not just bold in words but that we are bold in action also. Remember, God, prepares the table before us in the presence of our enemies. That's right; heavenly options are on the table. When the enemy attacks, we will use spiritual weapons and quite frankly, the divine power that is mighty in the pulling down of strongholds. We will demolish all the big talk and fictitious dreams of the enemy. Taking intelligence captive under the obedience of Christ. Then after we have completed this mission, we will be ready to deal with sin justly.

Galatians 2:21 I do not set aside the grace of God, for if righteousness could be gained through the law, Christ died for nothing!"

Dear friends,

There is great forgiveness for our sins through Jesus Christ by God's grace. But do not think this grace gives us a license to sin. No, no, dear friends. Do not take this grace lightly. This I can say, those who take this grace for granted become hard-hearted towards God, stiff-necked. Think about the nation of Israel which longed for the treasures of Egypt, they worshiped idols and often rebelled against God. Well, God's grace was so great toward the nation of Israel, but they overlooked His great grace. Now, this grace has become a stumbling block to that nation. But the grace of God has appeared to all people, and many say its foolishness. But it is salvation to those who believe in Jesus Name.

1 Corinthians 12:25 So that there should be no division in the body, but that its parts should have equal concern for each other.

Dear Friends,

Let's talk about Christ's administration. How does it work? Well in Christ's administration Jesus Christ is the Head of everything. All power and authority have been given to Him, and every member is part of that body. Every member is important. Regardless of person or position. God gives great honor to the lower members. When one member is inflicted the whole administration suffers, that much I can say, and when one member is honored the whole administration rejoices. It's equal opportunity and great honor with eternal benefits.

∫

Philippians 3:16 Only let us live up to what we have already attained.

Dear friends,

The next time that someone comes and says, I don't even believe that God would forgive a sinner like me. I've done way too many unforgivable things. Just look at them with great love and compassion and say, don't even think about it, forgetting those things that are behind and moving forward, press on toward the goal of the high prize in which Christ Jesus has called us heavenward. This means that we do not dwell on our imperfections. Jesus paid for our sins and bought our forgiveness. So, wherever sins abound, grace is even greater.

*Isaiah 59:19 So shall they fear the name of the Lord
from the west and His glory from the rising of the sun.
When the enemy shall come in like a flood, the Spirit of
the Lord shall lift up a standard against him.*

Dear friends,

Thanks be to God who has given us the victory through Christ Jesus who has paid for our sins. Don't even think about it. They have been forgiven. Now we will build a standard. That's right, we will build a beautiful standard, and we will keep in step with the Holy Spirit. Because when we live by the Holy Spirit, we do not gratify the flesh. It is when we get out of step with the Spirit that we become all fleshly, and we end up grieving the Holy Spirit. So, let us build this standard and watch the enemy tremble. Because he will not be able to come against our standard. Also, so important, let us rejoice! Not that the enemy cannot penetrate our beautiful standard, but that our names are written in the Lambs book of life.

Romans 8:3 For what the law was powerless to do because it was weakened by the flesh, God did by sending his own Son in the likeness of sinful flesh to be a sin offering. And so, he condemned sin in the flesh,

Dear friends,

Concerning these religious puppets. These so-called experts in the law and all their legalism. They are really bad for people and take advantage of innocent people. These fake ministers are only interested in one thing, and that is their own gain. They will not lift a finger to help any of God's people. They will not go very far before people figure them out. Jesus is the real deal. He cut through the legal tape and nailed down sin's policies to the cross. Then He rose above the failing power structures, condemning sin, He made a way by grace. Have faith in Jesus Christ's administration.

Hebrews 8:13 By calling this covenant "new," he has made the first one obsolete; and what is obsolete and outdated will soon disappear.

Dear friends,

Think of a card player. When someone is playing cards, and they think they have the best hand they are willing to put their money where their mouth is. But when someone is bluffing, and someone else calls them on it, they will be defeated unless they fold. Well, the devil knows that we are holding some weak cards and he wants us to fold. Even if we think our cards are good, they are never good enough. Because the devil plays with a stacked deck. But when Jesus holds our cards, it's a new and a better deal. All bets are off as grace appears.

Luke 11:52 "Woe to you experts in the law, because you have taken away the key to knowledge. You yourselves have not entered, and you have hindered those who were entering."

Dear friends,

I want to see the real deal in the church today. I'm tired of seeing fake Christianity. Know what I'm talking about, that shadow ministry that blocks everything that has the potential of enlarging God's Kingdom here on the earth. Those religious puppets that quench God's Spirit and keep His Kingdom from advancing. I'm tired of the hypocrisy. I want to see God's Kingdom come and His will be done here on the earth as it is in Heaven. That needs to be our prayer. For now, on it is Kingdom first. We will seek His righteousness and His Kingdom first.

Romans 14:17 For the kingdom of God is not food and drink but righteousness and peace and joy in the Holy Spirit.

Dear friends,

We are building a Kingdom, and it's a great Kingdom. It's the Kingdom of God. We are building His Kingdom here on the earth, which consists of righteousness, peace, and joy in the Holy Ghost. That's right, and it is the same Holy Spirit that equips us with giftings and abilities to fulfill this great responsibility, and it is a great responsibility. One that we cannot do on our own or by ourselves. We must have the Holy Spirit. So, give the Holy Spirit complete control and watch His Kingdom grow.

2 Timothy 2:25 Opponents must be gently instructed, in the hope that God will grant them repentance leading them to a knowledge of the truth,

Dear friends,

We must deal with sin masterfully but let us deal with the sinner with understanding and great compassion. Always keeping their best interest in mind. Remembering that God saved us while we were still sinners. We must try to put ourselves in their shoes. Do not judge them and do not grumble about one another. Take a kind and gentle approach. Allow the Holy Spirit to speak to their hearts. Now, this is so important; we must hate the sin but love the sinner. We know this. God is able to work a very bad deal into a very good deal with the repentant sinner.

Ephesians 4:27 And do not give the devil a foothold.

Dear friends,

When sin slithers in the doorway, and it wants to control our business, we must deal with it masterfully. This is the art of the deal. Not that we find a place to meet with that sin comfortably but that we make no room for sin in our lives. We will no longer give sin an opportunity in our company and never let sin be accepted in our workplace. Become sickened with its very presence. Its presence is sickening. If anyone, anyone has been dealing with sin wrongfully, they need to be ready to walk away from a bad deal. Sin is always a bad deal. So, give it to Jesus. He will set the person free. Then walk in that freedom.

1 Corinthians 15:57 But thanks be to God! He gives us the victory through our Lord Jesus Christ.

Dear friends,

Isn't it nice to win! Come on; it is so nice to win. Now, that's what we are. Winning people. For everyone, everyone who is born of God overcomes the world. The victory is ours. It is our faith in Jesus Christ that seals the deal. That's right, and it is God who made a way for us to be more than conquerors in Christ Jesus. So, everyone, everyone who believes in Jesus overcomes this world. He is in them, they are in Him, and He who is in them is greater than he who is in this world. Are we tired of winning yet? Well, Jesus tells us that those who are tired come to me and I will give them rest.

1 Corinthians 3:13 Their work will be shown for what it is, because the Day will bring it to light. It will be revealed with fire, and the fire will test the quality of each person's work.

Dear friends,

What does it mean if somebody says that cheaters never win? Well, it means that if someone is caught breaking the rules, there is no glory for that person. Now listen, Jesus Christ has redeemed us by His blood. A free gift by the grace of God. Whoever believes in Jesus will receive eternal life. But is a person winning if they are breaking the rules? Well, Jesus Christ will be the Judge of that. They may be saved but only as one escaping the flames of fire. There is no glory in breaking God's rules.

/

2 Corinthians 5:21 God made him who had no sin to be sin for us, so that in him we might become the righteousness of God.

Dear friends,

The world wants to strip away our wealth. Sin wants to leave us bankrupt. The devil wants to make us poor and powerless. But it's not going to work. For we are standing on great wealth in the righteousness of Jesus Christ. Not our own righteousness, which is but filthy rags, but the righteousness of Christ, which is more beautiful than diamonds. Even when we feel like we are totally spent, God's riches keep on flowing. In fact, it is when we feel like we are breaking that God can make us the richest. God can change that thing that we are wrestling with and make us shine like the noonday sun.

Hebrews 6:1 Therefore let us move beyond the elementary teachings about Christ and be taken forward to maturity, not laying again the foundation of repentance from acts that lead to death, and of faith in God,

Dear friends,

This is clearly the instruction and warning to grow in the wisdom and knowledge of our Lord and Savior Jesus Christ. The instruction is very simple. We are to continually add to our understanding of who Christ Jesus is, and become more like Him. The warning is that there is a very real danger of falling from the grace that has been given to us. Remember, it is by grace that we have been saved. Whether or not we can lose our salvation is up to God. But clearly, we can lose the Spirit of grace with whom we have been marked for the day of redemption. Without that deposit, we have no guarantee.

John 10:28 I give them eternal life, and they shall never perish; no one will snatch them out of my hand.

Dear friends,

What made the foolish bridesmaids foolish? Was it that they did not store up extra oil? Well, that was part of it but what about the fact that they left the bridal chambers? What about the fact that they went out in search of another source of power? That was a big mistake. Now listen, the devil wants to snuff out our fires. He wants to replace them with a strange fire so that the Lord does not even recognize us. Now please listen, this is so important when the light seems dim, and oil is low, stay in the chambers of God. Fire will fall, fresh oil will be poured out, and revival will come.

Acts 16:5 So the churches were strengthened in the faith and grew daily in numbers.

Dear friends,

Jesus Christ is building a Church, and it's a great Church, a mighty Church, a powerful, powerful Church. The gates of hell will not prevail against this Church. This Church will stand tall, and it will not fall. Because Jesus Christ is the center of it all. Every time that the devil tries to come against this Church, God will enlarge the Church. He will make it bigger and stronger. That's right, God is adding to the number of this Church daily. So, who wants to be part of this Church? This wonderful, beautiful, glorious Church? Then say yes to Jesus. Have faith in Christ. Let's make Jesus Christ our life!

/

Tell the devil no. God's people can't stop winning!

Colossians 3:4 When Christ, who is your life, appears, then you also will appear with him in glory.

Dear friends,

Who is truly living for Christ? Then live like a winner having entered into God's winning grace. But there is nothing sadder, no one more pitiable, than a Christian who has entered into God's winning grace, but they continue to live like a loser. Because that is what they are, a loser. When a child of God chooses to live like the devil, well let's just say, it is sad. Know this; a great victory comes with hard work. Well, God's grace has saved us, but we need to work out our salvation daily. Is Christ our life? Well then, live for Christ.

(

2 Corinthians 12:9 But he said to me, "My grace is sufficient for you, for my power is made perfect in weakness."

Dear friends,

Is there something in our lives that steals all our joy and it makes life just very difficult. Well, we know it came from the devil We prayed to God many times to remove the thing, but it continues to torment us. It's a messenger of Satan. A thorn in the flesh. Well, my thorn in the flesh is my speech. Quite frankly, sometimes I feel like the devil has got ahold of my tongue and I can't speak clearly. I think how I am ever going to be a preacher when no one can understand my speech. But when I humble myself before the Lord, and I glory in my weakness God's grace is great. It's an amazing win.

Romans 12:21 Do not be overcome by evil, but overcome evil with good.

Dear friends,

The enemy is getting so sick of us always winning, and he is trying to break up the fellowship between God's people so that we stop winning. But it's not going to work. We are going to walk in love and unity with one another. We are going to show people God's loving kindness which is better than life. Then because God's loving kindness leads people to Jesus. The devil will not be able to stand it. He might even say please, please, please, stop being so kind. It will be like heaping burning coals, hot coals upon his head and we will keep on winning.

Colossians 4:6 Let your conversation be always full of grace, seasoned with salt, so that you may know how to answer everyone.

Dear friends,

If we are going to be soul winners and win the souls of both men and women, that's right; this is for the women too, then we need to operate in the Holy Spirit. Now, the Holy Spirit is a gentleman. That means the Holy Spirit is gentle and tender. Kind and polite. The Holy Spirit does not lie. Well, a gentleman tells the truth. He knows honesty is the best policy. No half-truths and no compromise. So, be upright and be sincere, but always take a gentle approach. Be seasoned with the saltiness of our Lord Jesus Christ. Operate in the Holy Spirit, and we will know how to answer everyone.

1 Peter 5:6 Humble yourselves, therefore, under God's mighty hand, that he may lift you up in due time.

Dear friends,

Who wants to see some big wins? Remember Gideon? Well, Gideon was one of the early judges of the nation of Israel. When Gideon's army was strong God would not help Gideon's army least, they boast in their strength. It was when Gideon cut his army down to only three hundred men that God helped Gideon's army and gave Israel the victory. Listen now; when we think we are weak, then God will make us strong. God's power is made perfect in our weakness. So, don't worry about the enemy, just walk humbly before our God and win bigly.

2 Peter 3:1 But grow in the grace and knowledge of our Lord and Savior Jesus Christ. To him be glory both now and forever! Amen.

Dear friends,

Nobody, nobody deserves more honor and glory then, and we know who I'm talking about, the one who created it all. The one through whom all things are held together. For it is by His word that all things exist and without Him, nothing was made that has been made. He was and is and always will be. There is no one like Him. He is humble, lowly of Spirit and we could all learn from Him. So, let's put those hands together and make a joyful noise. Show the Lord our appreciation.

1 John 3:9 No one who is born of God will continue to sin, because God's seed remains in them; they cannot go on sinning, because they have been born of God.

Dear friends,

If we are going to win people, then we need to teach people to obey the word of God. It is a wonderful thing that God loves us, that He forgives us, and does not condemn those who are in Christ Jesus. Some are saved by God's great mercy all alone. But others need to be shaken to realize that God's great mercy came at a price. We can't take it cheaply. This means yes that Jesus died for our sins and we are forgiven. Now go and sin no more. Find the right mix. Because we are not winning people unless they continue on the winning path.

2 Corinthians 11:4 For if someone comes to you and preaches a Jesus other than the Jesus we preached, or if you receive a different spirit from the Spirit you received, or a different gospel from the one you accepted, you put up with it easily enough.

Dear friends,

It is time for God's people to lead from a position of strength. I understand the command to walk in love, peace, unity, comfort, and compassion. But dear friends, we are also commanded to rebuke with all authority. That means if anyone, anyone brings us another gospel, other than the Gospel of Jesus Christ let them be under God's curse. We don't need to bless them or say it's going to be ok because God is love. We know that God is love, but there is only one love that is inseparable, meaning no one cannot lose it. It is the love of God which is in Christ Jesus our Lord. Do not entertain destructive doctrine or policies.

Galatians 5:25 Since we live by the Spirit, let us keep in step with the Spirit.

Dear friends,

Let's talk about occupying every area, leaving no empty spaces. First of all, we need to identify the areas that we are planning to develop. The area I am referring to is the flesh. This is the ground that holds all those worldly desires and passions. We will strip away all the flesh and work with the infill of the Holy Spirit. The Holy Spirit will give us love, joy, peace, patience, kindness, goodness, faithfulness, gentleness, and self-control. The Spirit works wonders as we complete God's work.

Acts 3:19 Repent, then, and turn to God, so that your sins may be wiped out, that times of refreshing may come from the Lord,

Dear friends,

It's a movement. A movement of God. The movement of God upon the hearts of His people. The movement of God that begins with the gentle nudging of the Holy Spirit. It's a movement where God's people are humbly responsive to that gentle nudging with prayer and repentance. It's a movement where God hears the cries of our hearts and shows tender mercy, forgiving our sins, and healing our land. It's a movement that will take a nation from disaster to victory. It's a movement that we call revival.

1 Corinthians 15:51 Listen, I tell you a mystery: We will not all sleep, but we will all be changed—

Dear friends,

Are we ready to be taken up, raptured, to meet the Lord in the sky and be with Him forever? I'm talking about never tasting death. Quite frankly, it sounds crazy, too good to be true and it really can't be explained. It's like a surprise riddle. We have the facts, and we ponder them over and over again, but until the key is revealed, the secret remains hidden. The bible says that first the dead in Christ shall rise. Then those of us that are alive when Christ returns will be changed. With the last trumpet. In the twinkling of an eye. Mortal will be made immortal, the perishable, imperishable, it's a great mystery, and we're just going to have to wait to see how it unravels.

Acts 8:15 When they arrived, they prayed for the new believers there that they might receive the Holy Spirit,

Dear friends,

Now that we are a new creation in Christ Jesus, we are free to receive the infilling of His Holy Spirit. Now, this is very important. We need to fill up all the empty spaces. Not just the ones that everyone sees but the hidden one as well. Any space that is left undeveloped becomes accessible to the enemy and vulnerable to corrupt interests. Well, those corrupt interests bring in more destructive thoughts and destructive policies. They destroy the new creation. That's why, beginning immediately, we will occupy every area with the Holy Spirit. Leaving no empty spaces

2 Corinthians 5:17 Therefore, if anyone is in Christ, the new creation has come: The old has gone, the new is here!

Dear friends,

It's time; it's time, it's indeed time to repair the spiritual infill structure within the human soul. I'm talking about those spaces of time that exists within the human heart. With what are we filling our hearts? Too many people are filling their hearts with destructive thoughts and policies. They are crumbling. Others have wasted their time on selfish plans, which are also doomed to fall. But the master builder will repair these structures if someone will allow Him. If we give Him our heart, He will repair our souls, and He will construct a body that will last.

i

John 6:63 The Spirit gives life; the flesh counts for nothing. The words I have spoken to you—they are full of the Spirit and life.

Dear friends,

It's play and pay, play and pay. In other words, whoever plays with sin is going to pay for being a sinner. Whatever a man sows that he will also reap. If we sow to the flesh, we will also reap of the flesh, and we will reap corruption. But if we sow to the Spirit, we will reap of the Spirit, and we will reap eternal life. Therefore, say no to whatever belongs to that earthly nature. Those worldly passions. The works of the flesh. Walk by the Spirit and do not gratify the desires of the flesh.

ſ

Galatians 2:4 This matter arose because some false believers had infiltrated our ranks to spy on the freedom we have in Christ Jesus and to make us slaves.

Dear friends,

There is no doubt collusion in the church. I'm talking about imposters who have tapped their way into the body of Christ, bringing with them destructive policies. Well, these phonies and frauds are trying to strip away the freedom we have been given in Christ Jesus and keep us in bondage. They are working for the enemy. Do not be misled. It was the devil who had us bound with the old law, but Jesus set us free. So true, Jesus set us free. Then, He gave us His Holy Spirit so we could walk in that freedom. Do not return to the old law and do not grieve the Holy Spirit. Walk in that freedom and keep in step with the Holy Spirit.

Ephesian 6:12 For our struggle is not against flesh and blood, but against the rulers, against the authorities, against the powers of this dark world and against the spiritual forces of evil in the heavenly realms.

Dear friends,

Beginning immediately, we will implement a strategy to stand against the wiles of the devil, to resist the devil's evil tactics, and to put a stop to his wicked strategies. We will wear God's battle armament. The armor of God. With the Gospel of peace on our feet, and the truth around our waist. Our hearts will be protected by His righteousness and our minds with His salvation. We will be aware of the devil's devices and quench his fiery darts with our faith. We will counter his evil attacks with the word of God. We will become heavily invested in our relationship with God. Maintaining communication with all kinds of prayer. Because an investment in God is an investment in the men and the women that He seeks to save.

1 Corinthians 4:20 For the kingdom of God is not a matter of talk but of power.

Dear friends,

God wants to exalt us above our foes. He wants us to lift us over our enemies. He wants to move us from victory to victory, from triumph to triumph, from amazing wins to spectacular wins. So, be bold and be strong. Strong in the Lord and the power of His might. Strong in His mighty power. Let us go from power to power, from strength to strength, and be transformed from glory to glory. Let us advance the Kingdom of God. Come on; we can do this?

Galatians 1:7 Which is really no gospel at all. Evidently some people are throwing you into confusion and are trying to pervert the gospel of Christ.

Dear friends,

If we are going to be a victorious people, we need to repeal the devils lies that say "Hey, I got you covered." I'm talking about every invented doctrine of salvation apart from Jesus. These things are heresies, and they bring swift destruction on whoever believes their fallacy. We need to repeal them. We will repeal these false gospels and replace them with that true plan of salvation given to us in the Word of God. The truth of the Gospel of Jesus Christ. For salvation comes through no other.

Matthew 25:8 The foolish ones said to the wise, 'Give us some of your oil; our lamps are going out.'

Dear friends,

We may have entered a window of time where God's grace has been extended to us but don't think this means that the battle is over. No, now is not the time to rest. Now is the time to collect more strength and to store it up in heaven. Think about it. What happens if Jesus comes again and we are running out of fuel? We are low on power. Well, remember the parable of the ten virgins. Five were wise, and five were foolish. It didn't work out so well for those five foolish virgins. Sure, they were virgins, and that means they were pure, but they had no fuel. They were running out of oil, and therefore they were powerless. Let's take this time to store up the oil of His presence and become strong in the Lord.

Philippians 2:5 Let the same mind be in you that was in Christ Jesus,

Dear friends,

      Jesus Christ, the Righteous Judge, has gone home to be with the Father. Now God is looking for a few good and godly men and women that will continue in the mold of Jesus Christ. Well, I'm not here to make a list of men and women that I think will fit into this mold. But rather, I am here to encourage everyone simply to allow Jesus Christ to mold us. That's right, allow Jesus Christ to mold us. Become more like Him, like-minded, having the same attitude. Yes, put on Christ Jesus. Because it is His righteousness that breaks the mold.

Psalm 34:8 Taste and see that the Lord is good; blessed is the one who takes refuge in him.

Dear friends,

There is no greater feeling than waking up in the morning to a fresh cup of rejoicing. I mean, it's like praise the Lord! When I smell the sweet aroma of Jesus Christ just brewing it reminds me that this is the day that the Lord has made and I can't stop rejoicing. It's that rich, bold flavor of my Savior that gets my feet dancing. That's right, and the Holy Spirit keeps my feet in step all day long. Come on, let's taste and see that the Lord is good.

John 16:1 I have said these things to you to keep you from stumbling.

Dear friends,

Very important, yes, so important, that we pay the most careful attention to what Jesus is telling us. See, Jesus is telling us that this world is not going to like us. Many will even hate us. People are not going to be nice to us, and they will kick us out of their churches. Horrifically, some will even try to kill us. That's right; they will try to kill us. So why would Jesus give us this bad news? Well, He gave us the bad news to strengthen and toughen our commitment to sharing the good news. The good news that Jesus has already overcome this world. The good news that we too will overcome this world if we remain in Jesus.

Psalm 1:6 For the Lord watches over the way of the righteous,

but the way of the wicked leads to destruction.

Dear friends,

It is time for us to stop walking around with ungodly people. Do not; I said do not stand around and listen to sinners. God forbids, yes, God forbids, that we sit around and poke fun like a mocker. We are going to separate ourselves. Yes, separate ourselves from the swamp that is all around us. I'm talking about that massive weight of corruption that so easily entangles God's people. We are going to set ourselves apart and unto God. That's right; it's going to be God first. God first. Then whatever we do will prosper.

Matthew 5:17 "Do not think that I have come to abolish the Law or the Prophets; I have not come to abolish them but to fulfill them."

Dear friends,

It is important to notice that Jesus did not come to abolish the law or put an end to its requirements. No, the law is still in place. But what Jesus did was complete the legal and binding obligations of the law for us who cannot. He paid our premium. Then He replaced that coverage with His blood, providing eternal security at no charge. It's free for everyone who believes. The law is fulfilled and replaced. See, Jesus trashed the enemy's legacy or whatever legacy the enemy hoped to have. It's a better hope. A better covenant. It's a covenant of grace.

Colossians 2:14 He wiped out what the law said that we owed. The law stood against us. It judged us. But he has taken it away and nailed it to the cross.

Dear friends,

There was a promise of eternal coverage for every person who completed the requirements of the law. The problem was that no one could pay the premium. The premium was perfection. If someone missed one payment, the debt would pile up. Well, Jesus came and paid our debt in full. He replaced the law with faith. Oh, the law is still in effect. Jesus didn't abolish it, but He met its demands, when no one else could, ending the legacy of the law. Jesus fulfilled the requirements of the law and provided a better hope for eternal coverage. It's fulfill and replace.

)

Ephesians 3:16 I pray that out of his glorious riches he may strengthen you with power through his Spirit in your inner being,

Dear friends,

If we want to be strong people, then we need to be rich people. That's right, rich toward God. From whom all blessings flow. Rich toward God, who generously, He generously gives us His Holy Spirit. It is His Holy Spirit that fights our battles. It is His Holy Spirit that teaches us, His Spirit teaches us, the winning strategy. It is His Holy Spirit that warns us, His Spirit warns us, of oncoming danger and His Spirit will safely, safely bring us to His heavenly Kingdom. That's right; it is out of God's riches that His Spirit flows. We need to be rich toward God. For it is not by power, not by might, but by my Spirit, says the Lord.

/

Luke 24:53 And they stayed continually at the temple, praising God.

Dear friends,

We are going to start praising again. That's right; we are going to start praising. Praising the Lord and lifting His Name on high. For He is worthy. We will give Him the glory due His holy Name. That's right, we are going to start praising again, and we are going to make a joyful noise unto the Lord. For Praise is most beautiful and excellent to the Lord, that's right; our God is most pleased with our praises. When we start praising, well, it's amazing what praising can do. Walls will come tumbling down; the door will be open up, strongholds will be broken. That's right, and the enemy, when we start praising the enemy will shudder. That's right; the enemy will say "please, please, please stop praising but we're going to say no way. For we cannot stop praising the Name of Jesus.

2 Timothy 1:14 Guard the good deposit that was entrusted to you—guard it with the help of the Holy Spirit who lives in us.

Dear friends,

      Do good for one another and walk in love. Make a good deposit on a great investment. It is also so important that we know how to protect that good deposit. Yes, be as harmless as a dove and as wise as a serpent. Know this; the thief comes to steal, kill, and destroy. If we are not watchful, the thief may take away that good deposit that we have stored away. We don't want to neglect the gift or overlook the blessings and lose the reward. Be alert and self-disciplined. Know that our enemy is on the prowl. Remember that God has given us His Holy Spirit to secure that deposit.

Matthew 19:21 Jesus answered, "If you want to be perfect, go, sell your possessions and give to the poor, and you will have treasure in heaven. Then come, follow me."

Dear friends,

Now that we know about a great investment, we need to seek the things of God with all our heart, at any cost. This means that we do not waste any time. We need to prioritize God's worth in our life, above everything else, like a priceless jewel. We must stop at nothing to take hold of God's prize. Quite frankly, a good deposit is made by doing good works with a pure heart. That means that we love people even when people are unlovable. Love is pleasing to God, and He will reward that. Very important, a pure heart is absolutely essential in making a good deposit. God will accept no unclean thing. Remember, a good deposit is always going to cost something, but the best deposit will cost everything.

Matthew 6:33 But seek first his kingdom and his righteousness, and all these things will be given to you as well.

Dear friends,

How much of our lives are we willing to invest in the Kingdom of God? How important is it to us that we obtain the things of God? The things that are seated next to Christ Jesus, who is seated in glory. Well, there was a little boy who was playing the claw machine. That machine with the metal claw that reaches down grabs the toy and drops it out as a prize. Well anyway, this little boy was playing the claw machine, and there was a stuffed dinosaur in this machine that little boy just had to have. He must have gone through quarter after quarter trying to get that dinosaur. This I will say, we need to ignite the same passion within us to obtain the things of God. Because that little boy did not give up. Sure, he was well spent but when he went home, he was holding that dinosaur, and he had joy on his face.

Mark 4:35 That day when evening came, he said to his disciples, "Let us go over to the other side."

Dear friends,

I believe that Jesus wants to take us to a higher level. He wants to bring us into a place of total dependency and trust in Him. Trust, in Him alone. That means saying no to ungodliness and worldly passions. Living a self-controlled, upright, and a godly life in this present age. In other words, it's saying no to all corruption. As long as we allow the enemy to keep us paralyzed in fear, we are not going to see that miracle happen. But if we step into the boat and awaken Jesus, He will calm the storm, and He will increase our faith. Step into the boat. It's a movement!

/

We are winning the lost!

We are winning the world!

Ephesian 2:6 And God raised us up with Christ and seated us with him in the heavenly realms in Christ Jesus,

Dear friends,

We have a seat assigned to us in glory. That means that it is ours as long as we claim it. Or in this case, proclaim it. If some thief comes along and tries to steal our seat, we have two options. We can either crawl down and take a lower position, or we can stand up and say "that is my seat thief. Go back to where you came. It is so important that we understand that no one, NO ONE, can snatch it away from us. Sure, we can be a coward, and we can be afraid to stand up and take a lower seat. Revelation 21:8 makes it perfectly clear; the cowardly will be assigned a seat in a very different place. Remain securely seated in and with Christ Jesus.

2 Corinthians 13:6 And I trust that you will discover that we have not failed the test.

Dear friends,

The Apostle Paul tells us to test our faith and see that Christ Jesus is in us. Well, I have a question. Are good works evidence that we have passed the test or are bad deeds evidence that we have failed. Well, the devil would love for us to believe that we made an unforgivable mistake, but Jesus turns our mistakes into God's benefits. He turns our bad into God's good. If no one makes a mistake, if all their works are good, then they are a perfect man. Well, the apostle Paul prays that we all reach perfection, but until we reach perfection, we need to know that Jesus helps us with our weaknesses. Sometimes things seem so dark, and we feel like we made a mess of things. We feel like we've failed. Like we've failed at work. Like we've failed at home. Like we have failed at life. But we have not failed God. If we cry out to God, He will strengthen us, support us, restore us, and establish us. We will know that Christ Jesus is in us and discover that we have not failed the test.

Zechariah 7:1 "This is what the Lord Almighty said: 'Administer true justice; show mercy and compassion to one another.

Dear friends,

There were two brothers. They both belonged to the same household. Sons of one father. Both of them were good children and worked very hard to please their father. Each boy had a different perception of dad. One boy knew that dad was tender, kind, compassionate, and loved well doing. So, he walked heavily in love. The other son knew that dad was a strong disciplinarian and expected things done right. That boy tried to maintain justice. Nevertheless, both of them knew their father and both agreed that dad was great. Together they made quite a team.

James 1:4 Let perseverance finish its work so that you may be mature and complete, not lacking anything.

Dear friends,

What James is telling us here is that when we got those engines started, we want to kick it into high gear. We want to set it in overdrive and never look back. Always be moving forward no matter how tough the competition gets. We must put the ax to the grinder as we hit each bump. When the race seems difficult, we don't want to give up. No, that's when it is time to celebrate. Let the party begin. Because as we pass each checkpoint with perseverance, we will advance in the competition. Becoming stronger in character, refined, never missing anything.

2 Timothy 4:7 I have fought the good fight, I have finished the race, I have kept the faith.

Dear friends,

Paul gives us two images of someone who keeps the faith. The first image is of a prizefighter who blow by blow suffers pain and exhaustion. He may get knocked down, but by the power of Christ Jesus he gets up again. Now, the fight is almost over, and the adversary still stands, but Paul knows that he has pleased the Judge and the decision is his. Secondly, we see the image of a runner. Well, the runner is someone who also endures extreme difficulty and high fatigue, yet he continues to run the race according to the rules. That's right; every runner that crosses the finish line must continue moving forward no matter how hard the race becomes. If the runner wants to win, he must make every second count. Never give up. Never throw in the towel. Always be moving forward in the faith, redeeming the time. So that we win!

James 4:8 Come near to God and he will come near to you. Wash your hands, you sinners, and purify your hearts, you double-minded.

Dear Friends,

We have all overlooked God's blessing. We have neglected His gift. We have wasted his reward. Then when God stops blessing us, we repent and say I'm sorry Lord, please forgive me, and He is faithful, and He's just. He forgives us of all our sins, and He cleanses us of all unrighteousness. We are forgiven. But we still feel disconnected. Quite frankly, it's as if we have exhausted God and He has withdrawn from us. Well, no one can ever exhaust the love of God, and He will never leave, nor forsake us. So, if someone is feeling disconnected from God, the problem is not up there. The problem is right here. It is in our hearts.

2 Timothy 2:19 Nevertheless, God's solid foundation stands firm, sealed with this inscription: "The Lord knows those who are his," and, "Everyone who confesses the name of the Lord must turn away from wickedness."

Dear friends,

To build a strong faith, we need to begin with a solid foundation. Well, Jesus is the centerpiece of that solid foundation; Jesus is the Chief Cornerstone. Our faith is being built on that foundation. Our faith is built on nothing less than Jesus blood and righteousness. It is belief and confession that Jesus is Lord and that God raised Jesus from the dead, that is the core of our faith. But what is our faith-building? It is building the Church. Not a building being constructed by human hands but a people being raised up by the word of God. So, our faith adds to the Church daily. Our faith also teaches us that we are to leave this life of sin and turn to God. Our faith begins with belief and confession, and our faith remains faithful through obedience to God.

1 John 3:3 All who have this hope in him purify themselves, just as he is pure.

Dear friends,

John is writing about one of my most favorite messages. That message is preparing for the glorious appearance of our great God and Savior, Jesus Christ. This is a message we all need to hear, and we all need to embrace. This is a message of hope, of blessed hope. That we will all see Jesus, and when we see Jesus, we will be like Him. So, we wait for this blessed hope in eager expectation. Eager to see Him. Eager to see what we will become. Eager to see what He has in store for those that love Him. So, we make every effort to purify our hearts in preparation for His coming. Jesus promised us that it is the pure in heart that will see God.

1 John 5:21 Dear children, keep yourselves from idols.

Dear friends,

John is warning us about idols. Well, Paul makes it clear that an idol is nothing at all. So why the warning. Well, I don't believe it is the actual idol that John is so concerned about. I think that John's concern here is to be on guard from an idolatrous relationship. Now listen, an Idol divides a person's heart by weakening their devotion toward the true God. God wants to be first in our lives. Have no other gods before us. Anything that competes with God in the heart can become an idol. We must not let our love for God grow cold. Guard the heart. Because when the heart is split in two it causes even the strongest of Christians to fall.

Hebrews 11:6 And without faith it is impossible to please God, because anyone who comes to him must believe that he exists and that he rewards those who earnestly seek him.

Dear friends,

One of the most nerving situations is having to drive through a rainstorm in the dark. There is something very unsettling about not being able to see the road ahead. But there is an unusual trick to increase vision. Strangely enough, wearing polarized sunglasses makes the road becomes much clearer. Sure, it seems like foolishness, in the natural, but it really works. Well, in a similar way, there is a way to see clearly on the road to life. When it is dark out, and the rain is pouring. Look at things through the eyes of faith in Jesus Christ. The Spirit will give us a clear vision and navigate us through the storm.

Jude 1:24 Now to him who is able to keep you from falling, and to make you stand without blemish in the presence of his glory with rejoicing.

Dear friends,

Jesus is able to keep us from falling. That means that when we are tempted with more than we can bear faithful God provides a way out. But we have a responsibility; we must stand carefully on the word of God. To pay most careful attention to what we've heard and keep in step with the Spirit. Now, remember this, the love of God is our motivating factor. Say no to corruption. Seek first His Kingdom and His righteousness. God will provide a way out. No matter how strong that pull may be or how weak we may be, Our God is greater. Quite frankly, in the end, Jesus will have us standing upright in celebration.

Matthew 7:24 "Therefore whoever hears these sayings of Mine, and does them, I will liken him to a wise man who built his house on the rock,

Dear friends,

And we know the parable of the wise and foolish builders. It is that simple. The wise man builds His house upon the rock, Jesus is that rock. We must build our faith upon the teachings of Jesus Christ and stand firm on that foundation. Remember this, Jesus is able to keep us from falling. Let us be mindful of His word. Fixed on instruction in righteousness and godliness. So, the foundation will not be moved, and we will not fall.

1 Peter 1:13 Therefore, with minds that are alert and fully sober, set your hope on the grace to be brought to you when Jesus Christ is revealed at his coming.

Dear friends,

Do not let our minds wander from the truth in God's word. God's word is the standard that we need to live by. Let us renew our minds with God's word. Let God's word be our instructor. Let it convince us, correct us and instruct us in all righteousness. Know God's word and do what it says. God has given us the power to live a godly life, and it is in His word. Therefore, we will conduct our behavior according to God's word. Exercise self-control. In this way, we will please God and bear much good fruit. But what if we disappoint God? What if we break His command? What if we disobey His word? Well, that is all part of our blessed hope. That grace and truth came through Jesus Christ. That is not to say that there are no consequences for our actions. No, not at all, we will all stand before the judgment seat of Christ and receive what is due for what we have done in this body, rather good or evil. But this I will say, that grace will be given to Jesus Christ's faithful followers when He Is revealed. Hope in that grace.

Titus 2:12 It teaches us to say "No" to ungodliness and worldly passions, and to live self-controlled, upright and godly lives in this present age,

Dear friends,

Here we are at the bottom of the 9th. The Saints have a runner on 1st who says no to ungodliness and worldly passions. Self-control is holding up nicely on second. Righteousness is standing upright on 3rd. Now we have a godly life up to bat. Well, a godly life takes two strikes and steps away to talk with the coach. A godly life takes time out to get connected. A godly life says I can't do it, coach, I've come up short, the Devils have a real snake on the mound, he's got a wicked curve, I need power. The coach said, do not be afraid. I have given power from on high to trample on that snake. The victory belongs to this team. Just be patient and stand firm to the end. A godly life put his helmet on and hit a grand slam. The whole team cheered for him as he crossed home.

(

Proverbs 11:30 The fruit of the righteous is a tree of life,

and the one who is wise saves lives.

Dear friends,

Here we are, it's late in the hour and the Saints still need one to tie it and two to win. A godly life got connected which resulted in a grand slam, Now following a godly life is the evangelist. Well, the evangelist lays down some nice groundwork and comes off nicely with a double. That brings out patience who has no problem waiting for his pitch. Patience watches the first two pitches go by while the evangelist witnesses to second. The third pitch goes long and high on the outside. The fourth pitch goes deep and wide on the inside. Who can comprehend it? Well, the coach calls time out and gives patience a new bat. This bat says endurance on it. Now, patience has endurance and steps back into the box. Patience hits a high pop fly toward 2nd. The evangelist calls out repent and be saved. The second baseman trembles and drops the ball. The evangelist crosses home where the umpire declare He's saved. Then patience comes in with the winning run. All glory to God.

Galatians 6:3 If anyone thinks they are something when they are not, they deceive themselves.

Dear friends,

Now batting is one of the proudest of players, Sumting Arnot. Well, Sumting has a way of working the crowd. Sumting always makes a lot of noise. Sumting tries to scare the players by letting everyone know just how high and far he's going to launch the next pitch. Sumting wants everyone to think that he holds all the power. But Sumting never hits the ball. Sumting always strikes out. Sumting never brings the runners home. Therefore, Sumting never scores any points. That's what happens when someone believes Sumting Arnot.

2 Corinthians 5:6 Therefore we are always confident and know that as long as we are at home in the body we are away from the Lord.

Dear friends,

Where does our confidence lie? What are we confident about? What is the source of our confidence? Do not let our confidence be in our bodies or what we think we can do. Our bodies are just temporary dwelling places, and therefore, they have limitations. They are subject to loss and decay. But we have an eternal dwelling, and we shall receive new immortal bodies when we see Jesus. Therefore, be confident in the Lord and as long as we remain in this body, let our work honor and glorify the Lord. Then we shall always remain confident for God will never fail.

Matthew 5:37 All you need to say is simply 'Yes' or 'No'; anything beyond this comes from the evil one.

Dear friends,

Does this mean that if a Christian change their mind that they are listening to the devil? I don't believe so. Look at a parable Jesus told in Matthew 21. A father asked his son to go out in the field and do some work, but the son said no. The father asked his other son, and he said yes but he did not do it. Both sons were children of the same father and both sons knew what the father wanted. The one that said no changed his mind and did the will of the father. I don't think that kind of a mind change comes from the evil one. I think it comes from above. I believe Jesus is teaching us about the simplicity of our heart. Remain pure and honest and make no room for the devil.

(

1 Thessalonians 4:17 After that, we who are still alive and are left will be caught up together with them in the clouds to meet the Lord in the air. And so we will be with the Lord forever.

Dear friends,

We are about ready for departure; we will be taking off shortly. Please find a seat. Secure a position. Remain in Him. Make sure the seatbelt is on and that it is securely fastened. Set aside all baggage and put away all devices. Please, make sure the seat is upright and listen for the captain's instructions. In case of an emergency know, we're in good hands. Thank you for traveling on raptured airways. Where the result is great glory.

Philippians 1:29 For it has been granted to you on behalf of Christ not only to believe in him, but also to suffer for him,

Dear friends,

Paul reminds us that just as God has granted eternal life to all who believe in Jesus, He has promised eternal treasure to all who suffer for Him. Therefore, we need to walk worthy of the calling God has placed on our lives. That means we need to endure hardships and remain patient in the face of suffering. When temptations come, and temptations will come, it is our privilege, our advantage to be able to stand under it. For we know Christ and the power of His resurrection, share in His sufferings, and somehow partake in the resurrection of the dead. Also know this, that not all of us will fall asleep. A whole generation will be changed. I believe we may be that generation. What a privilege.

2 Timothy 2:21 Those who cleanse themselves from the latter will be instruments for special purposes, made holy, useful to the Master and prepared to do any good work.

Dear friends,

When a food critic visits a fine restaurant, they expect their food to be served on clean dishes. When the food is served on a dirty dish, it is immediately sent back to the kitchen. The whole meal is criticized as unfit for consumption, and the master chef becomes disgraced. Well, in a similar way, the world is evaluating our walk with Jesus. If we desire people to consume the spiritual food that God has given us, then we need to prepare our bodies to be instruments of righteousness, holy and pleasing to God.

Matthew 5:25 "Settle matters quickly with your adversary who is taking you to court. Do it while you are still together on the way, or your adversary may hand you over to the judge, and the judge may hand you over to the officer, and you may be thrown into prison.

Dear friends,

We need to make every effort to walk in love, even with our adversary. Sometimes love has to surrender its rights for the benefit of others. It is not an easy thing to drop some battle, especially when we feel that victory is ours. But love is the most excellent way. Love is most pleasing to God. Remember, God is love. I'm not saying that a Christian should compromise the truth, but sometimes we have to extend that olive branch. This is wisdom from God. Yes, act justly and love mercy and don't forget to walk humbly before God.

1 Corinthians 14:8 Again, if the trumpet does not sound a clear call, who will get ready for battle?

Dear friends,

This scripture is speaking of spiritual gifts and their proper use. There are many different gifts all by the same Spirit. Some of the gifts are meant to speak to the believer, and some are meant to be a sign to the unbeliever. A gift that speaks to a believer is often considered crazy or silly to the unbeliever, and the sign to the unbeliever is often discredited as indecent or disorder by the believer. Nevertheless, the real thing will awaken people or disrupt their comfort zone. The result is always that the gift will build up and edify the church.

Revelation 12:11 They triumphed over him

by the blood of the Lamb

and by the word of their testimony;

they did not love their lives so much

as to shrink from death.

Dear friends,

What happens when someone breaks faith with the Lord? When they fail to uphold God's holiness? This was the very reason that Moses could not enter the Promised Land. We all know the story. The people were thirsty. God said speak to the rock. Moses struck it twice. Those two blows spoiled his testimony. There is great power in the testimony of the saints. Our testimonies have the power to make us overcomers. Although we have spoiled our testimonies, God gave us new testimonies in Christ Jesus. Now we may enter the promise.

Psalms 125:3 The scepter of the wicked will not remain over the land allotted to the righteous, for then the righteous might use their hands to do evil.

Dear friends,

Who is excited to hear the voice of God? Because He is calling His people! The presence of the Lord is all over this earth. Yes, I know that God is omnipresent, but this goes beyond His abiding presence. I'm saying His power and majesty is here to reign in our lives. He wants to revive His church and save whoever has ears to hear. We are on the cusp of the greatest outpouring this world has ever known. Sure, the flesh screams for what it wants. Make no provision for the flesh. Disregard those cravings, thirsts, hunger, and appetites.

Romans 12:1 Therefore, I urge you, brothers and sisters, in view of God's mercy, to offer your bodies as a living sacrifice, holy and pleasing to God—this is your true and proper worship.

Dear friends,

The grace of God has brought salvation into our lives. We all know this, for it is by grace that we have been saved and not of works. Quite frankly, it is this same grace that teaches us how we should live while we wait for Jesus Christ our great God and Savior. It teaches us to say no to ungodliness and worldly passions. We are to live self-controlled, upright, and godly lives in this present age. In this present age! That means now, today. Not later when this age of grace is over. But live a life pleasing to God now.

John 15:8 This is to my Father's glory, that you bear much fruit, showing yourselves to be my disciples.

Dear friends,

Today I want to talk about increasing our net worth. Hopefully, we all know what we are worth in the sight of God. God holds us with tremendous value. We are precious in His sight. Each person is highly loved, greatly cherished, and crowned with glory and honor. But what is our net worth? If we weigh our assets against our liabilities where does one stand? Know this, that even one sin turns all our assets to liabilities? The God who created our original worth demolished our liabilities and raised our assets with Christ Jesus. Now, by living a life pleasing to God through faith in Christ, we may increase our net worth and be overjoyed with the gross income.

James 5:7 Be patient, then, brothers and sisters, until the Lord's coming. See how the farmer waits for the land to yield its valuable crop, patiently waiting for the autumn and spring rains.

Dear friends,

James gives us a very interesting picture here of patience from the hard-working farmer. There is no doubt that the farmer must observe the conditions of the land if he wants to reap those valuable crops. He will have to fight some wars and be on the alert for chaos. Nevertheless, the farmer remains patient, working the ground, confident that he will see the latter rain. Be patient. Do not grow tired. Do not give up. Get ready to reap for harvest time is near.

Acts 24:25 As Paul talked about righteousness, self-control and the judgment to come, Felix was afraid and said, "That's enough for now! You may leave. When I find it convenient, I will send for you."

Dear friends,

For two years Paul tried to persuade Felix, the governor of Rome, telling him why he needed Jesus. That he was not going to make it without Jesus. Jesus Christ is the way of righteousness that God requires. Jesus is the truth, teaching us self-control for godly living. Jesus is the life that escapes the coming judgment. But Felix would not listen to the wooing of the Holy Spirit. Well, two years went by, and Felix never made a decision. He continually sent Paul away. Listen, dear friends, Jesus is the way, the truth, and the life. Make a decision for Him today.

J

2 Timothy 2:3 Join with me in suffering, like a good soldier of Christ Jesus.

Dear friends,

We are not our own. We were bought with a price. Our bodies are the temple of the Holy Spirit. Therefore, we need to present our bodies to God a living sacrifice, holy and pleasing. Know this, God is well pleased with a pure and clean vessel, but God is most honored and glorified with a willing vessel. Be that willing vessel? Obedience is better than sacrifice. Let's commit our ways fully to our Commanding Officer.

We are winning the battle. Winning the war!

1 Peter 5:9 Resist him, standing firm in the faith, because you know that the family of believers throughout the world is undergoing the same kind of sufferings.

Dear friends,

We all are undergoing the same kind of sufferings. That does not mean that we all suffer to the same degree. No, one person may suffer much more pain than another. But there is one who has suffered in every way that we have suffered. He feels our pain and knows our hurt. He cares for us and promises to repay us with everlasting joy. If we remain patient in the face of suffering. Therefore, to whatever degree we do partake in these sufferings, consider it classified as light and momentary. Then we will be richly rewarded on that day.

James 5:16 Therefore confess your sins to each other and pray for each other so that you may be healed. The prayer of a righteous person is powerful and effective.

Dear friends,

There are two kinds of fireworks. There are those that sparkle, flare, and make a lot of noise and smoke. They are quick and easy to set up. They take little time to prepare and are relatively inexpensive. They are well grounded and do satisfy the immediate need. Then there is the kind that shoots up to the sky with big results. The second take time to prepare and can be a lot of work and planning. They usually come at a pretty hefty cost, but they benefit a great mass of people. Duds occur if the flame dies out and there is a failure to ignite. The spark must connect with the source for results. The results are always amazing.

John 14:12 Very truly I tell you, whoever believes in me will do the works I have been doing, and they will do even greater things than these, because I am going to the Father.

Dear friends,

Fireworks are the works of fire on a particular agent. Usually, that agent is gunpowder. The results are explosive and amazing. Similarly, explosive and amazing results accompany the works of Christ in the believer. Why? Because Christ went to the Father, but He gave us His works to finish. That's right, we are His workmanship, and we have been created to accomplish good works. So, we carry the works of Christ, and that workload is light. Why is that workload so light? Because Jesus holds the weight. Jesus also gave us an agent. That agent explodes into the miraculous. That agent is the Spirit of God living inside of us. So, we light the fuse by doing Christ's work, and when it meets the agent, God's Holy Spirit, the results are always amazing.

Galatians 5:1 It is for freedom that Christ has set us free. Stand firm, then, and do not let yourselves be burdened again by a yoke of slavery.

Dear friends,

On July 4th we celebrate our freedom as a nation, a wonderful, wonderful gift from God. But I want to remind everyone of the freedom we have from sin because of our Lord Jesus Christ. Now, 2 Corinthians, that's two Corinthians 3:17, and this is the whole ball game, that the Lord is Spirit and where the Spirit of the Lord is there is freedom. That's right; we are free from the power of sin when we walk in the freedom of the Holy Spirit. For the Holy Spirit gives us power. Now, we know this, with great power come great responsibility. Do not use this freedom as an opportunity to sin. It is our responsibility to keep in step with the Holy Spirit.

ʃ

2 Corinthians 8:9 For you know the grace of our Lord Jesus Christ, that though he was rich, yet for your sake he became poor, so that you through his poverty might become rich.

Dear friends,

Today I feel like I need to share the true prosperity gospel. How many of us would like to be wealthy? I mean well-to-do. Rich! I'm not talking about money, which plunges people into ruin and destruction. What does it profit a man to gain the world yet lose his soul? No, I'm talking about true wealth. The kind of riches that come from obeying the Father. Which we all fail to do. We all miss the mark. But thanks to Jesus we can be spot on or perfect and hit the mark. Surrender everything to God and follow Jesus. He will supply everything we need. He will make us rich toward God. Then we will have treasures in heaven. An eternal fortune.

Colossians 1:19 For God was pleased to have all his fullness dwell in him,

Dear friends,

When the stock markets crash, and the economy is tumbling. When the nations of this world are perplexed, and WWIII is on the horizon. When the environment is hostile, and the weather patterns have become unpredictable. When meteors, asteroids, and comets are approaching the earth and other heavenly bodies are entering our realm of existence. When there is global panic, and new world order is in the works. There's only one place one can turn. There's only one Name to call on. Jesus Christ, in whom the fullness of God dwells bodily. Turn to Him. He has the answers.

Luke 12:39 But understand this: If the owner of the house had known at what hour the thief was coming, he would not have let his house be broken into.

Dear friends,

A thief comes first to steal, and he has a plan to make it happen. An accomplished thief knows the objects he plans to take. He has a high appreciation for its worth. He is mindful of its value above other objects. His desire for that object is strong; the thief will become intimate with that object and will even design purposeful and strategic movements for that object according to his plan. Then when the time is right, when it seems darkest out, everyone is snuggled in their beds and feel safe. The thief will snatch that object away from the world. Similarly, the day of the Lord will come like a thief in the night. When it's dark out. When most people are spiritually asleep. When most of the world feels safe and secure. But it is a false sense of security for those who have ignored the lateness of the hour. That is when the Lord will snatch the object of His affection, a people that are His very own. Pay attention to the hour. Be watching, waiting, and anticipating.

Hebrews 11:40 Because God had us in mind and had
something better for us,

Dear friends,

Without faith, it is impossible to please the
Lord. No, it's true, because anyone who comes to God
must believe. First of all, that He exists. Second of all,
that He is the rewarder of those who diligently,
earnestly seek His face. Therefore, we are building up
faith. We are going to have great faith. A strong faith.
Our faith will be built on Jesus. Our faith is going to
look a lot like Abraham, Isaac, and Jacob's faith. It will
also look like Joseph, Moses, and the prophets. We are
going to have great faith. A solid faith. A beautiful
faith. Who's going to pay? I do not doubt it; the devil
is going to pay.

1 Corinthians 15:56 The sting of death is a sin, and the power of sin is the law.

Dear friends,

Much like a bumblebee, death has a sting except for death's sting is much deadlier. The sting of death is sin, and it causes pain and burning for all eternity. But Jesus has defeated the sting of death with His death on the cross. Sin's powerful sting is in the law, but Jesus fulfilled the law because He never sinned. Therefore, death has no sting for those who follow Jesus. Follow Jesus, and we will be saying, "Oh death, where is your victory?" "Oh death, where is your sting?"

Genesis 5:24 Enoch walked faithfully with God; then he was no more, because God took him away.

Dear friends,

There is a most notable connection between the mystery of godliness and the mystery that we call the rapture. True godliness is essential to partake in the glory that will be revealed. Not just a form of godliness that denies its power. No, for it is that same power that raises the dead that will also transform our mortal bodies. It is the resurrection power of Jesus Christ. That means that we must take up our cross daily and follow Jesus Christ. We cannot just be all around the cross; we must be on the cross. Living a godly life. Like Enoch, who walked with God and then he was taken. Or like Elijah, who was the perfect example of how a godly life suffers but is saved through faith in God by grace.

John 9:4 As long as it is day, we must do the works of him who sent me. Night is coming, when no one can work.

Dear friends,

We need to work hard at whatever it is that God has called us to do. Like a hard-working farmer, we need to make the most of the daylight because when the sun goes down work ceases. At nighttime, the hardworking farmer leaves the field and is welcomed at home with his valuable crops. But the lazy and disobedient farmer may spend the night in the field weeping. Weeping because he has no crops. Weeping because he's in the field where work has stopped. Weeping because his spouse has shut the door. Jesus tells us to work hard while it is the day because now is the time and the time is short. Do not waste time. Do not get left in the field.

1 Corinthians 15:23 But each in turn: Christ, the firstfruits; then, when he comes, those who belong to him.

Dear friends,

Paul's point here is that we have hope more than just in this present-day life. We have future and eternal hope. This hope is not just a dream or a wish. This hope is sure and steadfast. This hope is absolute. Quite frankly because Christ Jesus was raised from the dead, we have hope that God will also raise us from the dead when Christ Jesus appears. What if Christ Jesus appears in my lifetime? Well, then we will not need to be resurrected from the dead, but this same hope will transform our mortal bodies into immortal. This is our hope. This is the hope of glory, and it is only in Christ Jesus.

2 Timothy 1:6 (NKJV) Therefore I remind you to stir up the gift of God which is in you through the laying on of my hands.

Dear friends,

One of my most favorite cookies of all times is that of the chocolate chip. I remember when I was a kid making chocolate chip cookies. I remember adding the ingredients. Things like flour, sugar, butter, vanilla. I even remember putting an egg in the mix. Separately each ingredient served a purpose, but collectively they made one tasty cookie. Then, when we stir the chocolate chips, wow, we have a taste sensation. Well, in a similar way, individually, we are all necessary parts of the body of Christ, but collectively we form God's Church. That's a solid foundation. Now, mix in the gift of the Holy Spirit, and we have one sensational Church.

Philippians 4:9 Whatever you have learned or received or heard from me or seen in me—put it into practice. And the God of peace will be with you.

Dear friends,

Want to know a secret? This is the secret to end all life's pressure and stress. Ready for it? Only five words away from the ultimate anxiety releaser. Listen carefully, Rejoice in the Lord always. I will say it again, rejoice. I know what most people are thinking, Whatever. Yes, that's good. Now we're getting it. Whatever! Whatever is true. Whatever is right. Whatever is lovely. Whatever is pure. Whatever is noble, admirable, excellent, and praiseworthy. Think on these things. With prayer and thanksgiving. Then, the peace of God will guard our hearts and our minds in Christ Jesus. Amen

Philippians 2:4 Not looking to your own interests but each of you to the interests of the others. Jesus stopped

Dear friends,

One of Jesus most memorable parables is that of the Good Samaritan. I'm sure we have heard this parable before. A man got robbed and left for dead on the side of the road. He cried out, but no one seemed to care. Everyone was busy with their own concerns. Finally, a Samaritan, an outsider, a perfect stranger, he stopped and helped the man. Well, Jesus not only told this parable, but He also lived this parable. When He met a blind beggar, on the side of the road, and the man was crying out for Jesus to help him. Well, Jesus was busy, He was on His way to Jerusalem, but still, He took the time. He stopped and He helped the man. I am so thankful that Jesus stopped to help us when He went to the cross.

7\

John 20:26 A week later his disciples were in the house again, and Thomas was with them. Though the doors were locked, Jesus came and stood among them and said, "Peace be with you!"

Dear friends,

How many know the story of doubting Thomas? Well, I think that doubting Thomas represents a Christian who lacks any real resurrection power in their lives. They have locked the door on God in their hearts. They say that Jesus is Lord, but they have trouble grasping the truth that God raised Jesus from the dead. They know Jesus as crucified, and they still see Jesus as on that cross. They have heard the stories, they know the facts, but they still discount the miracles of today. Jesus does not want us to slam the door on these people. No, avoid foolish arguments, they only cause fights. It's like Jesus said, "Peace be with you." Watch Jesus appear even when the doors are locked.

Luke 21:19 Stand firm, and you will win life.

Dear friends,

We are all here today for one reason, and that reason is Jesus. Jesus delivers a message of true freedom, healing, and abundant life for all. His government never ends. His Name is perfect and blameless. There is victory in Jesus Name. Never be ashamed of that Name. Tell the world our testimonies and what Jesus has done for us. Let the world know where real and lasting hope is found. Hope that does not disappoint. Explain why this hope is in us and let the world know that this hope is available for everyone who believes in His Name. Become all things to all people that we might win some. But remember, it's not about the numbers, it's about the heart that is changed. So, remain patient and stand firm, Jesus will be here shortly.

Hebrews 10:35 So do not throw away your confidence; it will be richly rewarded.

Dear friends,

A school student can receive five different levels of honor in a typical grading system. An A, B, C, D, or F. If a student wants to be rewarded with an A, they must know the right answer. Jesus is the right answer for everything. Let our confidence be in Him and Him alone. There are many strategies to build strong confidence. A wise student makes it a habit to attend class and listen to the teacher. If a student is missing classes and ignoring the lessons, they are throwing away their confidence of an A. Sure one can scrape by with a C, or D, they will still advance, but there will be nothing to boast. Try to participate, be active, do the assignments, study the material, and don't be afraid to ask questions. The student who is well acquainted with the material remains confident. It builds their faith in the answer. Remember, Jesus is the answer. Have faith in Jesus and be amazed at the results.

Revelation 3:22 Whoever has ears, let them hear what the Spirit says to the churches."

Dear friends,

There are so many alarms going off in the world today and rightly so. We are living in the last days and the day of the Lord is at hand. The book of Revelation lays it all out, and it is pretty alarming. The world needs to hear God's alarm and wake up. But please do not be alarmed by the events that are unfolding today. Pay attention to these alarms but be anxious for nothing. These alarms are merely prerequisites to the Lord's soon return. God sounds His alarm amidst it all. He is telling His Church to wake up. To buy gold for the fire, white robes for their bodies, and salve to open their eyes. Otherwise, He will come like a thief, and they will not be ready. We must be prayed up, make our request known to God and be pure hearted. Walk upright, be full of the Holy Spirit, and excited about who is coming, not what is coming. Know this; we may escape all of that.

Isaiah 55:6 Seek the Lord while he may be found;

call on him while he is near.

Dear friends,

In the Old Testament Moses, told the Israelites to cast lots to hear from God. The idea was that God's will would be revealed through the results. It was not a game of chance, but an act of faith that God would provide a sign. God's purpose was never for His people to seek the sign, but to seek the Lord. Well, Israel began to seek the sign and missed the Lord's coming. Their hearts became hard. Jesus Christ came and performed many great signs and wonders, and His own did not even recognize Him. Well, we are living in the last days. We see the signs of the times. Let us not become hard-hearted and miss the Lord's 2nd coming. Remember the purpose of these signs is to seek the Lord. So, as we see signs of destruction, disaster, misfortune, trouble don't focus on a person's lot in life. Cast all those cares on Christ because He cares.

1

2 Corinthians 6:1 As God's co-workers we urge you not to receive God's grace in vain.

Dear friends,

Do not let God's grace be wasted. Could it be any clearer? We are all guilty of this very thing. I'm not talking about neglecting the gift or overlooking His blessings, which we all have done too. No, I'm talking about wasting His rewards. Salvation is a gift from God through faith. Through faith in Jesus Christ, we all received one blessing after another. We may receive the gift of the Holy Spirit. This is all by the grace of God. But God's grace does not stop there. His grace is eternal toward His children. Therefore, let this extended grace become greater in each of us.

John 3:36 Whoever believes in the Son has eternal life, but whoever rejects the Son will not see life, for God's wrath remains on them.

Dear friends,

God's wrath is currently being reserved for judgment. Which means that no person alive has experienced it. I want to point out that God's wrath was experienced in the days of Noah. The next time God's wrath will be released will be the end of days. Jesus told us it will be as it was in the days of Noah and unless those days were cut short no one would survive, but for the sake of the elect, those days will be cut short. Praise God! He has us in mind, and He has something better for us.

1 John 5:3 In fact, this is love for God: to keep his commands. And his commands are not burdensome,

Dear friends,

Who ever heard the song Jesus loves the little children? What is it about the little children that Jesus loves? Is it their faith? That they are full of belief and are obedient to dad. Well, that is part of it, but I think the bigger picture is a little child's heart is selfless and full of love. They do what dad says without grief. The child needs no reward or incentive. Knowing dad is smiling is satisfaction enough. It's when they become teens that they want the stereo, tv, cars, money, or something else to get the job done. They start thinking that if they don't get what they want, then nothing is going to get done. Everything is a burden. Then it's some big surprise when dad gets it done by himself, but he's not smiling. I think Jesus loves the little children because the little children walk in obedience to dad, and even more, that it's not a burden.

Psalm 94:19 When the cares of my heart are many,

your consolations cheer my soul.

Dear friends,

When a contestant loses on a game show, often they will be given a consolation prize. This means that the contestant has lost and is eliminated. They have been labeled runner up. Another name for these consolation prizes is parting gifts. The purpose of these gifts is to keep the player happy while they exit the stage. All their worries and anxieties are temporarily calmed. Well, dear friends, God's consolations do more than calm the mind and body. They cheer the eternal part of a person, the soul. They give us joy. Not temporary relief but joy everlasting. No longer labeled runner up. In Christ Jesus, we have been declared winners and are moving forward. In glorious triumph. We are given a second chance. By His grace, we receive chance after chance. Every time we fall, He is there to pick us up again. Now parting is no longer sweet sorrow but eternal joy.

Hebrews 10:39 "But we are not of those who shrink back and are destroyed, but of those who believe and are saved."

Dear friends,

I feel the Spirit is asking us all a question here. The question is a simple one. What are we going to do? This question is not aimed at mocking us. The Spirit is not saying that it's hopeless out there, we did what we could, but the darkness increases. We better just accept it and worry about ourselves. No, worry will get us nowhere. Jesus said, which one of you by worrying can add a single moment to their life. So, what will we do? Will we shrink back or press in? This question is not to taunt us, but to spur us on. It is to challenge us to go deeper!

)

Psalm 31:22 In my alarm I said,

"I am cut off from your sight!"

Yet you heard my cry for mercy

when I called to you for help.

Dear friends,

What is the purpose of alarms? Warning people, scaring people, waking people up, these are all effects of an alarm but what is the alarm truly for? An alarm is for the purpose of telling people that now is the time. An alarm clock tells people it's time to get out of bed. An oven timer tells people it's time to get that cake out of the oven. A burglar alarm tells people it's time to attend to and protect their house, money safe, car, etc. So, what is the purpose of the alarm in the human heart? It goes off when someone is facing that which opposes God. It is telling them it's time to get up. It's time to get out. It's time to protect our souls. It is telling them to turn around and leave that thing. It is telling them that now is the time to return to God. Do not write it off as a false alarm. Listen to the heart. Run to the mercy seat and cry out to God. God will silence that alarm and bring peace.

1 Timothy 6:14 To keep this command without spot or blame until the appearing of our Lord Jesus Christ,

Dear friends,

Timothy has been charged, ordered, directed to keep this command. What command? The command to walk as Jesus walked. Well, how did Jesus walk? He walked in the way of love. Timothy has been instructed to do this perfectly. Without spot or blame. Just as Jesus told His disciples to be perfect as our heavenly Father is perfect. In other words, we need to be faultless. Whether we believe we can achieve this or not, it is our command. We must be excellent at what is good and innocent of evil. We must pursue the things of God. Imagine that we are digging for treasure and the more dirt we remove, the more gold we uncover. Now, remove the dirt from everyday life and expose the gold which is refined by fire. For our, God is a consuming fire. Yes, be excellent at what is good and rich in good deeds. Then when Jesus appears, we will be richly rewarded.

John 15:19 If you belonged to the world, it would love you as its own. As it is, you do not belong to the world, but I have chosen you out of the world. That is why the world hates you.

Dear friends,

Jesus has chosen us out of this world. That means we are going to see things differently. From a different perspective. From God's perspective. We are going to do things differently too. Because we are not of this world. Sure, we are in this world, but we don't seek the things of this world and worldly desires. Those things will not last. They are passing away. We seek the things of God and God's desire. The will of the Father. The same person that Jesus aimed to please and the world hated Him. They kicked Him out of the place of worship and crucified Him. Thinking they were doing God service. Now, Jesus warned us that a time is coming when the world would treat His followers the same way. I think that time is now. But don't go astray. Be bold. Be strong. Be patient in suffering. For it is the person who does the will of God who lives forever.

1 John 3:8   The one who does what is sinful is of the devil, because the devil has been sinning from the beginning. The reason the Son of God appeared was to destroy the devil's work.

Dear friends,

Sometimes God's people do the wrong thing, and it is sinful. Does that mean they are of the devil? No, the child of God might end up doing the wrong thing, but they are a doer of the will of God. That person looks intently into the word of God. Quite frankly, when God's children become aware of sin in their lives, they turn from it, repent. They are forgiven, but the apostle John tells us the very reason that the Son of God appeared in human flesh was to put an end to sin. So that the people of God may resist the devil and he will flee. He must flee. Why because the Son of God appeared in human flesh and died in our place. By making our lives subject to Christ's death, we may know the power of Christ's resurrection. Ultimately attaining the resurrection from the dead unto eternal life. As God's beloved children make no room, give no place to the devil. He's been undone!

Philippians 3:3 For it is we who are the circumcision, we who serve God by his Spirit, who boast in Christ Jesus, and who put no confidence in the flesh—

Dear friends,

Why would we put no confidence, zero, zippo, zilch, in our flesh? Because, there is nothing, nil, naught, in our human bodies that will save us. Not our beauty, muscles, brains, physical abilities, heritage... This part of man is temporal. It is here today and gone tomorrow. The spirit of a man is eternal and therefore seeks eternal things. This is the part of man that may truly discover Christ Jesus. So do not trust and satisfy that part of man that is designed for death. Live in the Spirit and unearth the eternal, for the eternal is not of this earth.

John 19:30 When he had received the drink, Jesus said, "It is finished." With that, he bowed his head and gave up his spirit.

Dear friends,

We have been entrusted with the privilege of releasing this Gospel to the world. It is a privilege because God has chosen us out of the seven + billion people in the world, to display and convey Jesus' Name with our actions. We should be ready and excited to do what is good and innocent or blameless of evil. There is a great reward for those who willingly and joyfully let their light shine. There is nothing left for us to do but receive eternal life. Just open our hearts and receive love and forgiveness. It is finished.

We will win the high-prize.

We will win life.

2 Timothy 3:1 But mark this: There will be terrible times in the last days.

Dear friends,

It appears that we will be experiencing some turbulence on this journey. Do not wander off in search of anything. Please stay calm and remain seated. The captain will supply all our needs. The Captain has warned us that we are headed into some turbulent times. But if we continue in the faith, rooted and built up in Christ Jesus, God's power will bring us safely out of that rough patch, and we will be in the sky in no time for God is faithful. On behalf of the Captain, I want to say thank you for exercising patience endurance as we continue to travel towards our destination. Remember this, the very hairs on our heads are all numbered.

Revelation 19:9 Then the angel said to me, "Write this: Blessed are those who are invited to the wedding supper of the Lamb!" And he added, "These are the true words of God."

Dear friends,

A father was working on paying the bills when his beloved son enters the room. The son asks his dad if he will throw the football with him. Dad says, "Not right now. I have to pay these bills." Then the son went and sat down by his dad, but never said a word. He just sat there and watched his dad. Well, dad got irritated being watched and said: "Go, watch tv and I'll play football with you later." The son said, "I don't really want to play ball or watch tv. I just want to be where you are." Know this If we ask for bread, will He give us a stone? If we ask for a fish, will He give us a snake? If we can sincerely say to God, "I just want to be where you are," He is not going to deny us. He will welcome us in His presence!

Joel 1:15 Alas for that day!

For the day of the Lord is near;

it will come like destruction from the Almighty.

Dear friends,

Everyone loves a great comeback. No, I'm not talking about a snappy response to an insult. I'm talking about the presumed underdog overcoming life's troubles and challenges to become victor and champion. Well, when Jesus first appeared it was as the presumed underdog. He was rejected and put to shame. His own did not even recognize Him. They declared Him unfit. He rose up to life. He overcame the opposing forces. He won the battle royal and holds the most exalted title, King of kings and Lord of lords. Still, this world refuses to acknowledge His title. His own continue to look for another. One that their fathers did not even know. Jesus Christ will return and show the world who is boss. So, let all who have ears to hear say come, Lord Jesus, come.

1 Corinthians 1:7 Therefore you do not lack any spiritual gift as you eagerly wait for our Lord Jesus Christ to be revealed.

Dear friends,

If we are truly eager to see His glorious appearing, it is going to show in our actions. Eager people are not passive. They are aggressive. Like a sports fan. They are going to make some noise. Well, let's make some noise for Jesus, in eager expectation, by being excited to serve Him. Yes, serve the Lord with gladness. As the body of Christ, we do not lack in spiritual gifts. We have all been given different gifts. Do not let the gift remain idle. Fan it into flame. In other words, exercise the gift. By doing this, we speed Jesus great and glorious coming. As if that is not enough, we also speed the revealing of what we shall become. For we know that we shall be like Him. So, let us be eager to do what is good as we hasten that day.

Philippians 3:20 But our citizenship is in heaven. And we eagerly await a Savior from there, the Lord Jesus Christ,

Dear friends,

Imagine being on a road trip. Think of a little child who loves, trust, and respects their father. They are very excited to reach the destination, but they remain calm, without complaining, enduring the hardships of the journey. Always looking forward with longing and desire to behold the coming attraction. As the end draws near anticipation grows. They see the signs and eagerly ask the father, "Are we there yet?" Father says, "Almost, just a little while longer." They see more signs, and again, the child says "Daddy, are we there yet?" Dad says, "Not yet but soon and very soon." That eagerness may cause that child to ask five, ten, fifteen more times, but they never lose heart, because they know daddy is going to get them there.

1 Corinthians 1:8 He will also keep you firm to the end, so that you will be blameless on the day of our Lord Jesus Christ.

Dear friends,

This truth goes so much deeper than our present-day troubles. I believe this promise gives us future hope. Listen, there is a time of great tribulation coming on this earth. A time when temptation will be more than we can bear, more than we can handle, for God will remove the Spirit of grace and release a spirit of strong delusion. But God is faithful! When we are tempted with more than we can bear, He will provide a way out. That way out is not so that we can stand under unbearable temptation without sufficient grace. The way is removal so we can stand before the Son of Man. Have faith in Jesus. He will keep us firm and secure. We will be found blameless and worthy to escape all that is coming. Quite frankly, I do believe we will escape all that is coming.

2 Corinthians 1:10 He has delivered us from such a deadly peril, and he will deliver us again. On him we have set our hope that he will continue to deliver us,

Dear friend,

This is the assured promise that God will rescue us from every evil attack. He will safely bring us to His heavenly kingdom. That deliverance is a guarantee for those who are in Christ Jesus. To those who have placed all of their hope in Him. This is our sure and definite comfort. Not only has God delivered us from sin, death and the consequence of hell. He continues to rescue us from whatever tries to bind and chain us. That's right, from deadly peril, from a lethal threat, from the fatal blow. So, we have set our hope on Jesus. That hope will not shame us. It does not disappoint us. For we have more than just the comfort of hope in this life. We have the certainty of knowing that the same power that raised Jesus from the dead will give life to our mortal bodies. Amen, Amen, and Amen.

Philippians 1:10 So that you may be able to discern what is best and may be pure and blameless for the day of Christ,

Dear friends,

Jesus is coming back for His Church. Now very important, without holiness no one will see the Lord. I'm not talking about observing Him with the natural eye, for every eye shall behold His glorious appearing. I am talking about seeing Him with our spiritual eyes. The eyes of our hearts. When God opens the eyes of our heart, we see the Lord Jesus. We walk in the light, and the blood of Jesus Christ cleanses us from all our sins. It is He who makes us holy not ourselves. Sadly, if we stop walking in the light, we lose discernment, and our vision becomes clouded. We end up losing focus and become impure and guilty. Thank God for His Holy Spirit who convicts us of guilt and gives us discernment. So, we know when we are walking the wrong way. When we are off track. So, walk in the most excellent way. The way of love. Walk in the light.

J

Philippians 1:6 Being confident of this, that he who began a good work in you will carry it on to completion until the day of Christ Jesus.

Dear friends,

I want to go on the record today saying that I am nothing without my God who is everything. I know that, if I am willing to go, He's faithful to show. He's not finished His good work in me. Now, whenever I think, that's it, no more God, I'm done, God is disappointed with my faithlessness, and I become unfruitful. Know this, when I say, I got nothing God, but here I am, God is faithful, and He takes me to the next level. He confirms His word is true and He blesses me for obedience. He has promised me that He will continue to do so, until the day of Jesus Christ. I can say no and miss the blessing. Quite frankly, why would I want to do that? Now that I have tasted and I've seen that the Lord is good. I'm not saying that salvation depends on works. Faith in Jesus saves us. Just don't think that God's good work won't be accomplished by some other willing person who is hungry for the blessing. Be eager to do what is good and know that God is still working.

Ecclesiastes 12:1 Remember your Creator

   in the days of your youth,

before the days of trouble come

   and the years approach when you will say,

   "I find no pleasure in them"—

Dear friends,

      Spend every free moment tiptoeing to that quiet place just be alone with Jesus. I use the word tiptoeing because it is a time of secrecy. We need to be almost sneaky about it. Not deceitful but discreet. Life is busy and there is always something that needs to be done. Finding that intimate time with the Lord can easily lose precedence. Take time to get connected. Let's make that our top priority each day. Seize, capture, take command over every pocket of time to simply worship Jesus. Slip away and say breathe on me, Master! For the days are increasingly evil. In order to redeem the time, we must spend time with the Redeemer.

*Romans 16:25 Now to him who is able to establish you
in accordance with my gospel, the message I proclaim
about Jesus Christ, in keeping with the revelation of
the mystery hidden for long ages past,*

Dear friends,

I will say it again, we need stability in these last
days and it needs to come from God. Not from worldly
riches or possessions. Not from the government or
any other power. Our stability must come from God,
and it must be in agreement, in harmony, in sync with
the gospel of Jesus Christ. Listen, God is not only able,
but He wants to establish His people. Does anyone
realize what that means? It means that He will make
us steady and strong. He will form and create stability
in our lives. Yes, He will create stability in our lives,
and we will not be moved, we will not be shaken. He is
our firm foundation. We will trust God to create
stability in our lives today and find our secure position
in Jesus.

Daniel 3:25 He said, "Look! I see four men walking around in the fire, unbound and unharmed, and the fourth looks like a son of the gods."

Dear friends,

We need stability in these last days. We can't have one foot stepping out in faith and the other foot staggering back in doubt. It's not going to work. I'm not talking about salvation. I am talking about the people of God, His called, His chosen, taking their stand against the evil of this day. Not backing down. Like Shadrack, Meshach, and Abednego, when they faced the fiery furnace. They made a decision. They faced the trial. They declared, rather God saves them or not, they will not waiver or change their minds. They would not serve a false god. Suddenly, Jesus appeared in the fire. We need that kind of faith to face the fiery trials of these last days.

Revelation 16:15 "Look, I come like a thief! Blessed is the one who stays awake and remains clothed, so as not to go naked and be shamefully exposed."

Dear friends,

This verse is a wonderful promise amid great judgment. It promises that the church has nothing to fear. For it will be caught up to meet the Lord in the sky. It will be snatched away from great tribulation. It is this very verse that tells us to look and behold, I come quickly, in a moment, in the twinkle of an eye, and my fierce anger will be poured out. Woe, to the inhabitants of the Earth. They will not be ready. That day will not come like a thief to my church, to the people of God, for they are watching and waiting. They are dressed and ready to go. They are eager to do what is good. They are blessed. They will not be there to suffer my wrath but will inherit salvation. Call it escapism or say I'm daydreaming, I don't care. It is what it is. Quite frankly, when reality hits. It's what God has promised, and God can not lie.

Hebrews 10:29 How much more severely do you think someone deserves to be punished who has trampled the Son of God underfoot, who has treated as an unholy thing the blood of the covenant that sanctified them, and who has insulted the Spirit of grace?

Dear friends,

Under the law, God's loving mercy was available only to those who received the law. The lawbreaker who disregarded the law received no mercy but only just punished. An eye for an eye and a tooth for a tooth. Now grace has appeared and offers salvation to all people. Grace has extended God's mercy to whosoever believes in Him. Who's Him? Only one, Jesus Christ. It is God's loving mercy that keeps us from receiving what we deserve, namely death. Then God's grace gives us what we do not deserve, eternal life. It's by grace through faith. This means that when we make a mistake, and we all make mistakes, God's grace still covers us. Now, if we deliberately go on sinning, it is no longer a mistake. To live that way is denying Christ Jesus' Lordship in our lives. Do not trample on this grace.

2 Corinthians 13:5 Examine yourselves to see whether you are in the faith; test yourselves. Do you not realize that Christ Jesus is in you—unless, of course, you fail the test?

Dear friends,

We are instructed to conduct a personal and individual examination of our faith journey. To survey ourselves with a personal spiritual check-up. Make sure that our faith in Christ is alive and active. That Jesus has indeed risen from the dead and He lives in us. To get out our bibles and probe the motives of our hearts. There is no better tool to locate the weakened, damaged, or infected sections. Check the tree, inspect the fruit, and eliminate any parasites. Parasites are not flesh and blood. Parasites are rulers, authorities, powers, and the spiritual forces of heavenly places. Remember this; it's ok when we don't have the answer. When the test gets tough. When the solution seems impossible. Be happy! Be glad! Rejoice! It's the testing of our faith that produces endurance.

1 Corinthians 13:13 And now these three remain: faith, hope and love. But the greatest of these is love.

Dear friends,

In the mathematical world of division there are three parts to every problem. These parts have names. The dividend, which is the part divided. The divisor, which is the part that divides the dividend. Thirdly, the resolution, which is the end unit or the answer to the problem. Think of this world as the dividend and the mystery of God as the divisor. For God will divide this world between believer/unbeliever, godly/ungodly, righteousness/wickedness. Well, when Jesus comes, the mystery is revealed, and the problem of sin is resolved. Now, the imperfect will be destroyed; it will pass away. What will remain? Faith, hope, and love. I call these parts the remaining factors.

Matthew 7:18 A good tree cannot bear bad fruit, and a bad tree cannot bear good fruit.

Dear friends,

This is a word to the house of God. The believing body of Christ. The Church. Get out of the miry clay. A good tree cannot bear bad fruit. Although a good tree cannot bear bad fruit, a good tree can be fruitless; they can bear no fruit. What happens when a good tree becomes fruitless? Well, the Lord is patient, loving, merciful, and kind. He will continue to look after and care for His own. He will address the issues and nurse all problem areas. Then, He will give that tree time to heal. When the time is over, He expects to see some good fruit. For, in the end, every tree that does not bear good fruit is cut down and thrown into the fire.

1

Matthew 7:18 A good tree cannot bear bad fruit, and a bad tree cannot bear good fruit.

Dear friends,

A bad tree cannot bear good fruit. Why, because God's seed does not abide in them, and if they want to bear good fruit, they must plant good seeds. Only one is good, and that is God. The seed within us is at constant battle with God's seed of righteousness. What a poor victim we have become. The good we want to do, we cannot. Thanks be to Christ Jesus who gave us the victory when He carried our sins to the cross. He suffered and died on that cross for our sins. He set us free and won the war when He rose again. If we want to be a good tree, we must believe in Jesus. Believe that He is the Son of God. Believe that God raised Him from the dead. Then we will produce good fruit and receive eternal life.

1 Peter 2:2 Like newborn babies, crave pure spiritual milk, so that by it you may grow up in your salvation,

Dear friends,

Ever seen a baby with its bottle of milk? What happens when someone takes a bottle away from a baby. Well, the baby becomes very fussy, inflexible, and unyielding, as they cry out for more. Try to replace the bottle or substitute it. They spit it out of their mouth or push the substitute away. They do this because they have tasted what's good. This is how a baby grows up. Well, Peter tells us to crave the things Such as things that nurture our salvation. The good things of God; things that are true, noble, right, pure, lovely, admirable, excellent, praiseworthy. Yes, think about these things. Let the word of God be the standard by which we filter all things. Also, so important, get rid of anything that might pollute the mind and spoil this spiritual milk. This will result in healthy growth.

Hebrews 5:14 But solid food is for the mature, who by constant use have trained themselves to distinguish good from evil.

Dear friends,

This is a call to maturity. It's a good thing to crave pure spiritual milk. But once we start growing, like any baby, we're going to get some teeth. When a baby starts teething, they start chewing on solid foods. Not that milk is no longer needed, but it becomes a beverage to wash down strong meat. Sure, milk still strengthens the bones, but solid food is required for strong muscular development. Babies need muscles if they are to start walking. It is so important that we start walking out our faith. That we grow mature. That we are able to discern what is good, what is best. That we are able to walk in God's acceptable and perfect will. Anything less than God's perfect will may be unacceptable and therefore, get burned up. Continue to grow.

John 14:1 "Do not let your hearts be troubled. You believe in God; believe also in me.

Dear friends,

Welcome aboard flight 3:16. That's John 3:16. For God so loved the world that He gave His only begotten Son, that whosoever believes in Him should not perish but have eternal life. This is a non-stop flight to meet the Lord in the sky and to be with Him forever. Now the captain, our captain, Jesus. He has gone on ahead of us, to prepare a place for us, so that where He is, we may also be. He has told us not to be worried or troubled by this. He has not abandoned us or left us alone. He has asked His Father to send us a helper. Now, His Father did not hesitate to give us the Holy Spirit. So, buckle up and expect some turbulence. Also know this, that He has made us more than conquerors. This, I will say, we will reach our destination. Praise God!

J

Hebrews 10:25 Not giving up meeting together, as some are in the habit of doing, but encouraging one another—and all the more as you see the Day approaching.

Dear friends,

Can we see that day approaching? Not presidents or Election day. The day of the Lord. The day when Christ will gather His Church and they will be with Him forever. The Lord is coming when no one expects, but we can be ready. Are the days becoming more and more evil? Is wickedness increasing, wars being discussed, and violent acts being carried out? Has knowledge increased and technology exploded? Have we seen these things and other things taking place? Sure, we have, now here's what to do. Get in a solid, Spirit-filled, bible believing, holy living, fellowship driven church. We need to be joined with people who encourage us to look up. So that Day does not surprise us, like a thief.

Luke 15:31 "'My son,' the father said, 'you are always with me, and everything I have is yours."

Dear friends,

When the prodigal returned home, the older brother refused to welcome him. He was not happy about the situation at all. He felt cheated, overlooked, and jealousy overtook him. As a result, he became hard-hearted and grieved his father. Don't build distance from the Father. Have a heart for the lost. He wants no one to be lost, but for all people to come home. So, come to the party. Come to the show. Bring a brother. Bring a sister. Bring a friend. Rejoice and be glad for the Father is pleased to give us the Kingdom.

Hebrews 3:14 We have come to share in Christ, if indeed we hold our original conviction firmly to the very end.

Dear friends,

We have all taken a major test. Maybe it was at school, at work, for a job, or even a driver's test. The answer seemed clear, but we second guessed it when we read the other choices. When corrections are made, we failed. No retakes, no do-overs. Sadly, there is a feeling of loss after such a foolish mistake? No diploma. No job or promotion. No driver's license. If only we did not change that answer. Dear friends, as important as that test may have seemed we moved on. It wasn't the end of the world. Know this, a day is coming when we will all be tested by God and all our work will be tested. The decisions we make today will affect our eternal destiny. It will be the end of this world. If we know Jesus Christ, we know the right answer, Jesus is the right answer. Don't change the answer. Hold on to that original conviction.

/

Acts 4:12 Salvation is found in no one else, for there is no other name under heaven given to mankind by which we must be saved."

Dear friends,

There is an expression, a figure of speech often used when something is so important, so essential, so vital to life, that we have not lived until we experience this. The expression is it's a must. Grandma's Apple pie, that new action movie, the new sports club? It's a must. Well, there is no salvation apart from Jesus. There is no forgiveness of sin without His blood. There is no peace without the payment for our sins. There is no hope of eternal life without the Lord. Get saved, become born again, live for Jesus. It's a must.

2 Timothy 2:4 No one serving as a soldier gets entangled in civilian affairs, but rather tries to please his commanding officer.

Dear friends,

What happens when a solder disappoints the commanding officer? There is hell to pay. The worse the disappointment, the worse the punishment. Well, the truth is that we have all disappointed God for we have all broken His commands. God ranks all people the same. He has no favorites. All transgression receives its just punishment. Sadly, the just punishment is literal hell, where there are weeping and gnashing of teeth. But we can escape this punishment by full surrender and repentance to the Son of God. Because He paid our penalty and bought our freedom. This was all done while we were still sinners because God loves us. Therefore, like a good soldier, join me in the suffering of Christ and say no to the ungodliness. No, to worldly passions. Such things become a stronghold.

/

2 Timothy 2:5. Whoever enters an athletic competition wins the prize only when playing by the rules.

Dear friend,

We need to play by the rules for that's the way the boss wants it. The government's rules and the rules of those in authority, but above all by God's rules. God has given us these rules in His holy word. I'm talking about living a blameless life. A life without reproach. People will still point their fingers at us, but their accusations not stick. They may even tell lies, but God will expose them all. I know, it sounds like a handicap, a disadvantage. Quite frankly, when the truth comes out, they are the one with the spot on their names. We will be richly rewarded. So, don't be hard headed and say, I know what the bible says but I don't believe that applies to me or today. Play by the rules and have faith in Jesus, who always plays by the rules.

2 Timothy 2:6 The hardworking farmer should be the first to receive a share of the crops.

Dear friends,

It's going to take hard work, and it's not an easy road. Contrary to what people believe, the Christian life, It's no joy ride. Like a farmer, we are going to have to do some digging. We are going to have to remove some dirt. We are going to have to plant some seeds and care for them daily. But the good news is that the pain, the troubles, the sorrow may last for a night, but joy comes in the morning. We will reap when harvest time comes if we do not give up. Are we seeking a harvest? Well, it's hard work. It's a labor of love. It's seeds of faith working through love. God takes note of love. Love is what keeps God's attention. Love is what God rewards. God is love and everyone that loves is born of God and knows God.

1

James 1:25 But whoever looks intently into the perfect law that gives freedom, and continues in it—not forgetting what they have heard, but doing it—they will be blessed in what they do.

Dear friends,

"Are you talking to me? Are you talking to me? I know you're not talking to me." This is a famous scene from an old movie. I think that many of us play this role. When we read the word of God but do not do what it says. We open our Bibles, and God speaks clearly to us. Then we close our bible and say, Is God talking to me. Yes, God is talking to us. He is speaking through His word. He wants us to look intently into the holy scriptures for our flaws, weaknesses, and things that we need to correct. God will reveal these things to us if we ask. Pray search my heart and know my thoughts. Lord, see if there be any wicked way in me. His word will lead us in the way everlasting.

Titus 2:6 Similarly, encourage the young men to be self-controlled.

Dear friends,

Let me be clear about the way we need to operate. We need to obey the command and set restrictions on how we operate. Not our restrictions, but God's. That means we need to say no to what is wrong, and yes, to do what is right. This includes attitudes. We are to have the same attitude as Christ who is humble and selfless. Not selfish but selfless. Regarding others more important than oneself. We must take control of our mind. Don't think about worldly things. They are passing away. We need to be able to think straight. Set our minds on things above. Take control of our bodies. Make our bodies subject to Christ, through life in the Spirit. Put to death the misdeeds of the body. Lest we are led astray by the error of lawless people and lose our own stability. We must be self-controlled at all times. When we are being watched, and when we think we are alone. In season, and out of season. We will be righteous, spotless, blameless, and ready to meet the boss.

Hebrews 2:1 We must pay the most careful attention, therefore, to what we have heard, so that we do not drift away.

Dear friends,

There was a sea captain who had many honorable vessels. He gave instructions to make sure that each ship was properly tied to the dock before entering the port. Well, one of the crewmen was distracted by the waves of the ocean and failed to pay the most careful attention to the captain's instructions. When they reached the shore, he anchored the boat but never tied it to the dock. When he came back the next day, the boat was gone. The man panicked as he saw the boat in the distance drifting away. When he finally recovered the boat, he found that the anchor never let go. The ship just needed to be properly grounded. In a similar way, Jesus will never let go, but we need to be properly grounded, so we do not drift away.

We are more than conquers in Christ Jesus!

Colossians 2:19 They have lost connection with the head, from whom the whole body, supported and held together by its ligaments and sinews, grows as God causes it to grow.

Dear friends,

What happens when a Christian gives any less than 100% of their worship or devotion to God? At some point, they become disconnected from the head, which is Jesus. It's not that Jesus has left them. It is that they have lost their attachment. Because no one can serve two masters. That's a dangerous place to be dear friends. To become disconnected from the Head will seriously stunt all spiritual growth. In fact, it will stop, cease, and even prevent any further growth. God loves us too much to let us stay the same. He cares for us too much to leave us in the mess we are in. Stay connected.

Luke 12:20 "But God said to him, 'You fool! This very night your life will be demanded from you. Then who will get what you have prepared for yourself?'

Dear friends,

Many people have made this mistake before. They have fallen into this trap. They prepare for life's immediate needs and neglect the spiritual. Sure, they may be prepared to meet the mortgage, car loan, creditors, bosses, doctors, even the IRS. Are they prepared to meet God? Maybe they have done some incredible things. They are rich in good deeds. God has used them in mighty ways. Will, that alone prepare their soul to meet God? No, it might bring them a great reward and it might not. It all depends on how well they know the rewarder. Isn't He the rewarder of those who diligently seek Him? Jesus told us to seek His kingdom first and His righteousness. Not to worry about tomorrow, tomorrow will care for itself. Whoever wishes to save their life will lose it. Yes, we need to be watchful, alert, and ready for that evil day. Quite frankly, the thing we need to be prepared for is to meet God., to stand before the Son of man.

Psalm 119:27 Cause me to understand the way of your precepts, that I may meditate on your wonderful deeds.

Dear friends,

Today I want to talk about stretching boundaries and breaking the resistance toward the things of God. God wants to stretch our interpretation of His Holy Word. So that we no longer discount the bizarre Well, stretching can be a painful process. Stretching involves extending our comfort zone to break the resistance. Come on, think about it. Someone who works out each day has less resistance to stretching than someone who does no exercise. They can do straddles and splits with little resistance. Why? Because they push their physical limit every day. When a less active person struggles to touch their knees. Also, the less resistance a rubber band has, the farther it can stretch. Well, God wants to stretch us to break that resistance. So, our bodies, minds, and spirits are flexible to the move of God and responsive to His Word.

Psalm 42:1 As the deer pants for streams of water, so my soul pants for you, my God.

Dear friends,

Ever been in a relationship and hurt or disappointed the other. Maybe said or did some things without thoughtful consideration. The bond seems broken. Their affection seems far off. If only they would forgive. Remember the desperate determination we feel to see that relationship restored? Dear friends, what makes us think that God is worthy of any less devotion? If we confess our sins, God is faithful and just to forgive us, and to cleanse us. Because His forgiveness and His grace are so great, we forget that God is a relational being. He desires closeness, friendship, and intimacy. He opposes the proud but gives grace to the humble. Draw near to God, and He will draw near. It's daily walking close to thee.

1 Thessalonians 4:1 As for other matters, brothers and sisters, we instructed you how to live in order to please God, as in fact you are living. Now we ask you and urge you in the Lord Jesus to do this more and more.

Dear friends,

"Living to please God," that is my heart's desire. I make it my aim to find more and more ways to do so. I want to cause a beaming smile to blossom on the face of the One who my spirit just can't smile without Him. For it is His Spirit that breathes life to my spirit   I desire to be a light in this world of darkness, shining forth with the message Jesus is alive. I want to be the flavor of my Savior, the seasoning that lost souls unknowingly crave. I want to work with God's rising agent. The leaven of Heaven. That means I must become more and more dependent on Him. I'm obliged to empty myself of all filth, yet fortunate enough to become the aroma of Christ. I want to be a fragrance that is fully pleasing to God. Bringing Him joy. Making Him smile. That is where I find my strength.

Psalm 31:24 Be strong and take heart,

all you who hope in the Lord.

Dear friends,

Too many Christians are trying to duck and take cover when God has instructed us to be strong and take heart. I'm not asking anyone to step out and fire, but please stand up, stand up for Jesus. Our faith is being stripped away from us because people are afraid to stand. We live in dark and uncertain times and the word tells us that many will abandon the faith. Proudly, we are not one of the many, we are one of the few, the chosen, the elect. We are ambassadors of Christ. We bear His Name and we are protected by His blood. He has commanded His angels to guard us. He has given us authority over the enemy. Be strong and stand up.

Revelation 3:7 "To the angel of the church in Philadelphia write: These are the words of him who is holy and true, who holds the key of David. What he opens no one can shut, and what he shuts no one can open.

Dear friends,

Find a seat because the show is about to begin. I'm sure we have all heard this statement before a big movie or some type of show. Unless the viewer wants to miss the show, they pay attention. If they know the show is going to be a good one, they quickly find their seat and become focused on what is coming. Well, in a similar way, we are told by Jesus to be good watchmen or viewers of the events that are taking place in the world. Not to participate in them. Neither should we fear them. These things must happen, but please, keep our eyes open to interpret them. Also, when we see these things, we know that our salvation is near. Listen, this is not a movie, find a seat in Christ and stay focused on who is coming. Because once the door is closed no one is going to get in.

)

James 2:19 You believe that there is one God. Good!
Even the demons believe that—and shudder.

Dear friends,

Who are the demons mentioned in this
scripture? I do not believe James is talking about
disembodied spirits or ghosts. I believe he is talking
about the sons of God or fallen angels. For they once
lived with God and know His mighty power. They were
deceived by Lucifer and fell from grace. There was no
opportunity for repentance. They were denied
forgiveness. They received no further grace. Further
grace has been given to mankind through faith in Jesus
Christ. We have the opportunity today to repent and
turn from our wicked ways. We can be forgiven. Jesus
Christ became a man to save man, not angels. Do not
neglect so great a salvation. Act now!

Galatians 6:9 Let us not become weary in doing good, for at the proper time we will reap a harvest if we do not give up.

Dear friends,

Just a quick word of encouragement today. "Do not give up." Do not throw in the towel. We need to continue this race. There are no exceptions, and there are no outs. There is no fine print attached to this scripture that reads unless ... The life lived in Christ is not easy. Don't wander on easy street. For "difficult is the way that leads to life." Maybe the offer looks better over there but know that God has placed each person where they are. He has a plan for them. It's when we see no answer, yet continue to endure, that God makes things happen. He's hope for the hopeless. It's going to take patient endurance and much perseverance to run this race to the finish. We can do it because God is on our side! Know this; nothing is too difficult for God. With God all things are possible. So, get back up. Get back up. For harvest time is near!

1 Thessalonians 5:17 Never stop praying.

Dear friends,

What do people do when something breaks or stops working? They ship it back to the manufacturer or creator for repairs, with a detailed note attached. Why, because they don't have what is needed to fix the problem. Quite frankly, no matter how smart or capable we think we are. We can't fix this problem. This problem of sin that is in our world. Now, Jesus paid to fix this problem on the cross. Those of us who believe in His blood know this. What about the unbelieving world? We need to give it to the Creator with our prayers attached. Remember this, that Jesus is coming again, and He will repair all things. So, we cast our cares on Him for He cares for us.

2 Peter 3:1 Dear friends, this is now my second letter to you. I have written both of them as reminders to stimulate you to wholesome thinking.

Dear friends,

Let me inspire each person to wholesome thinking and hopefully awaken some to the reality of God. God revealed Himself in these last days through His Son, who this world rejected and crucified. That was two thousand years ago. Life has gone on normal ever since. Just as Christ said, it would. But then things would get strange. Knowledge would increase, Hearts would fail them from fear of what was coming on the earth. The nations would rise against Israel. The true church would be persecuted. These things are happening now. We are in the last of the last days. The labor pains are moving quickly. Get right with the Lord. Get right with the Lord. The time is short. Get right with the Lord.

Revelation 1:6 And has made us kings and priests to His God and Father, to Him be glory and dominion forever and ever. Amen.

Dear friends,

Welcome to Double-TW airlines, that's out of this world airlines. The transport to eternal dwellings. The transport of kings and priests. A ticket has been bought and paid for by the blood of Jesus. To Him be glory both now and forever, amen. We will be meeting this Jesus in the sky and be with Him forever. We are going to want to leave all the baggage behind and please set aside all carryon items. They will only weigh us down. We are not going to need them where we are going. It is time to get serious about our relationship with God and mean serious business. Because this flight is about ready to take off and we don't want to miss it.

Titus 2:11 For the grace of God has appeared that offers salvation to all people.

Dear friends,

If I could have everyone's attention for one moment, please. There are still seats available in the grace of God. Whoever desires to be seated in His grace let them come now. For it is by grace that we have been saved, and it is by His grace that we are here today. We will be boldly approaching our destination. The throne of His grace. In which we have received direct access through faith in Jesus Christ by grace. It's grace upon grace, one blessing after another. By the way, to each passenger grace is given as Christ distributes it. Do not ignore this grace, or set it aside, or fall short and miss it. This is the true grace of God, stand fast in it and may the grace of our Lord Jesus be with us.

Galatians 5:10 I am confident in the Lord that you will take no other view. The one who is throwing you into confusion, whoever that may be, will have to pay the penalty.

Dear friends,

It started as a friendly journey, and the road seemed right. Every turn I made worked wonderfully. Then I hit a bump, and it got me all disoriented, mixed-up. That's right, confusion hit, and I made a lot of wrong turns. When I realized I was lost, backtracking seemed impossible. I had gone too far and was too tired to remember how I got here. I felt scared and powerless. I knew If I kept going, I was going to run out of gas. So, I stopped my car and cried out to God. Help me, Lord. Then this amazing peace and clarity came over me. All confusion was gone, and God showed me the way out. Thank you, Jesus.

2 John 1:8 "Watch out that you do not lose what we have worked for, but that you may be rewarded fully."

Dear friends,

We are living in dark days. Anti-Christ and deceiving spirits are among us. Let us run so that we may win? We are warned to be on guard, so we do not ruin our testimony, and become disqualified from the prize. Who realizes the seriousness of disqualification? Disqualified means to be declared unfit and deprived of any consideration. In short, they lose for what they have worked. Does this mean they lose their salvation? No, I don't believe so, for we are not saved by works, but by grace through faith. Sadly, when someone loses their work. Well, let's just say it is sad. "Watch out that we do not lose what we have worked for, but that we may be rewarded fully."

J

Revelation 2:25 Only hold on to what you have until I come.

Dear friends,

The enemy wants to steal our reward, and not so he can have it, but simply to destroy it. He wants to see all our works burned up. God desires to reward us. Jesus longs to greet us with a big smile and say, well done good and faithful servant. Listen, we are His workmanship. Skillfully and wonderfully made. What happens when a product does not work? It brings shame to the creator when his work is ruined. We have been created for good works in Christ. Good works in Christ produce good fruit. Good fruit produces the eternal reward. Do not grow tired in doing good but wait patiently for that future glory!

Matthew 15:19 For out of the heart come evil thoughts—murder, adultery, sexual immorality, theft, false testimony, slander.

Dear friends,

Jesus told us a parable of the word of God being planted in the hearts of men. He used the illustration of seeds being planted in the different types of soil. There was shallow ground, rocky ground, and thorny ground. Each ground had its issue. It could not hold on to what it had received and was fruitless. The issues of life flow out of the heart. Do not let our hearts get weighed down with partying, drunkenness, or the anxieties of life. For suddenly, that day should close in on us like a trap. Let's set our minds and hearts on things above, and that is where our treasure will be.

)

Acts 4:13 – "When they saw the courage of Peter and John and realized that they were unschooled, ordinary men, they were astonished and they took note that these men had been with Jesus."

Dear friends,

What was it about Peter and John that was so remarkable, so outstanding, so noteworthy? It was not their education, power, or wealth. It was not their appearance or good looks. It was simply that they had been with Jesus. They had spent time in His presence. This was made clear by the confidence and openness by which, they proclaimed the Gospel. They were not hiding anything or keeping secrets. The people were impressed, even astonished by their transparency. Their lives were a living sacrifice, holy, blameless, and acceptable to God. Be careful not to misrepresent and cause others to stumble.

/

Romans 15:13 May the God of hope fill you with all joy and peace in believing, so that you may abound in hope by the power of the Holy Spirit.

Dear friends,

Hope in Jesus will not disappoint or shame us. Because our hearts are filled with the love of Jesus. That was one of the first things different about me when I gave my heart to Jesus. All the anger, resentment, bitterness, hate. They were gone! All the shame, disappointment, and condemnation. They were gone too. For there is now no condemnation for those, who are in Christ Jesus. Truly, that hope is not simply wishful thinking. Like oh, I hope it doesn't rain today. Or I sure hope to win that new car. It is sure and confident. Steadfast and active. Because it is rooted in love and love always hopes. Even against hope. Let the love of God fill our hearts with hope and be blessed!

Matthew 24:24 For false messiahs and false prophets will appear and perform great signs and wonders to deceive, if possible, even the elect.

Dear friends,

A man was coming home after a long day. He was tired and just wanted to rest. Well, he came up to a sign that read road closed. There was a sign to the right which read detour. So, he followed the detour sign believing it would get him back to the main road. Well, the signs took him right and left and all over the place. He must have traveled over an hour and was lost. Out of desperation, he cried out "Help me get home Lord." What does someone do when they are traveling all alone. They come to a sign that reads road closed. They take the detour trusting that it will bring them back to the main road. Well, in the natural that's what someone would do. They follow the signs. In the Spirit, we look for the signs but follow God. My point is this: don't follow the signs looking for God, follow God and watch for the signs. God will safely bring us Home.

1 Thessalonians 5:8 But since we belong to the day, let us be sober, putting on faith and love as a breastplate, and the hope of salvation as a helmet.

Dear friends,

Are we eager to do what is good? Do we hunger and thirst for righteousness? If not, then something is wrong with our salvation. I am not saying that our works save us, good works are not going to give anyone eternal life, but they certainly do verify, and give witness to, the fact that we belong to Christ. He is in us. They are our testimony. Our defense, our hope of salvation. Our helmet of salvation is made up of two elements. The blood of the Lamb, which is what Christ has done for us, and the word of our testimony, which is what Christ is doing in and through us. By them, we will overcome these dark days. Know them by their fruits. A good tree does not bear bad fruit and vice versa. All I'm trying to say is, check the tree.

Romans 8:1 Therefore, there is now no condemnation for those who are in Christ Jesus.

Dear friends,

The Holy Spirit will convict us of guilt in regard to sin, righteousness, and judgment, but it is someone else who puts a label us. Whether that label sticks, or not, depends on the judge, and every man will face God's judgment. If God sees our guilt, then we are forever condemned. Thank Jesus He bore our guilt and suffered our transgressions. It is because of Him that we can boldly approach the throne of God, on the day of judgment, knowing we are not guilty.

Psalms 29:4 The voice of the Lord is powerful;

the voice of the Lord is majestic.

Dear friends,

The Lord is calling out loudly in these last days! The voice of the Lord is over the waters. The voice of the Lord is over the troubled waters of our heart. Deep calls unto deep. The God of glory thunders. The God of wonder echoes. The voice of the Lord shakes the desert. His voice is shaking our hearts. Wake up and strengthen what remains. The voice of the Lord strips bares the forest. He wants to purify and make us holy. God reigned on high over the great flood, and He will reign forever. Majestic is the voice of the Lord. God's voice will command the final trumpet. Powerful is the voice of the Lord. Hear the voice of the Lord. It's time to pay attention and bring glory to His Name.

Luke 12:35 "Be dressed ready for service and keep your lamps burning,

Dear friends,

Quickly, there are three things that we need to do in preparation for the glorious appearing of our great God and Savior, Jesus Christ. First of all, we must be dressed, so that we are not found naked and shameful. This means that we must be clothed with Christ Jesus. We must be found in Him. Not having a righteousness that is our own, but one that comes through faith in Him. Second, we must be ready for service. This means we must be a living sacrifice, holy, and acceptable to God. Remembering it is not I who live, but Christ Jesus who lives in me. Thirdly, keep those lamps burning. This clearly means to walk in love and stay in step with the Spirit. Do not let that passion die down and that fire goes out. For once again, we know that the Lord will come like a thief in the night. We need to be prepared so that we may be worthy to escape all that is coming. Be sober-minded and think about it.

John 15:5 I am the vine; you are the branches. If you remain in me and I in you, you will bear much fruit; apart from me you can do nothing.

Dear friends,

We need to be fruitful for God and His kingdom. Fruitfulness is more than good works. A person can do good works all day long and still be fruitless in regard to eternity. The fruit of fruitfulness is the works we do, but the fullness of fruitfulness comes from abiding in Christ. Remaining in Jesus. The only way to remain in Jesus is by active faith and living hope. Also, most important, one must walk in the love of Christ. If we do these things, we will bear much good fruit, and we will make God smile.

Luke 10:11 'Even the dust of your town we wipe from our feet as a warning to you. Yet be sure of this: The kingdom of God has come near.'

Dear friends,

A law enforcement officer may write a ticket for speeding or missing the stop sign. He is not swayed by excuses no matter how reasonable or important they may be. He is going to write a ticket and tell that person to slow down. He may even say, "pay attention to the signs. When someone speeds like that they eventually end up dead". After such an encounter with the law, a person is sure to tell others. Well, it's time to stop ignoring the warning signs and tell others. Tell everyone! Tell them about the penalty for disobedience to the law, which eventually leads to death. Tell them about the warning signs. Most importantly, tell them about Jesus.

2 Thessalonians 2:9 The coming of the lawless one will be in accordance with how Satan works. He will use all sorts of displays of power through signs and wonders that serve the lie,

Dear friends,

I have been encouraging everyone to seek the mystery of Godliness, true Godliness. Have nothing to do with the counterfeit. For there is a counterfeit, and it is a mystery. It's the mystery of sin, lawlessness, the mystery of iniquity. It appears like godliness, but its power is not from God at all. Its power is based in lawlessness. It is rooted in the lawless one. The worker of iniquity, who works all signs and lying wonders according to the power of Satan. Sin appears powerful, mysterious, and even attractive. Do not be lured or enticed by Satan's so-called dark secrets. They are shameful even to mention. Instead, expose them, and blow the whistle on the devil. Do not fear him who can only kill the body. Fear Him who can kill the body and destroy our souls in hell. Let those who have ears hear.

1 Peter 1:3 Praise be to the God and Father of our Lord Jesus Christ! In his great mercy he has given us new birth into a living hope through the resurrection of Jesus Christ from the dead,

Dear friends,

We have all been in relationships. Some really great relationships. Where communication was a joy, and every word that person said was cherished. Every word that person spoke was so valuable. That person made us feel like we were the one and only one for them. Sadly, as time went on, that person began to take that love for granted. We continued to woo that person. Never ceasing to express great love for that person. Unfortunately, that person stopped expressing their love in return. It may have begun great in the beginning, but without love it became nothing. See, Jesus expressed the greatest love when He gave His life. Truly, it did not end there. He was raised from the dead. He continues to give love, and His Spirit continues to woo us. Do not take this great love, this amazing grace, for granted.

2 Corinthians 5:13 If we are "out of our mind," as some say, it is for God; if we are in our right mind, it is for you.

Dear friends,

I have no worries about looking foolish, and so what if the world doesn't understand. I'm not a minister to score cool points with anyone. I am not after their superficial love. I am compelled by that love which is better than life. My lips will praise Him. My heart will bless Him. I will lift up my hands, shout for joy, dance in circles, do handstands, and whatever else might appear humiliating for Him. I will be made the spectacle of the universe so that His name is lifted higher. The crazy thing is that when I do humble myself, He just lifts me higher. Better than life!

2 Peter 1:3 His divine power has given us everything we need for a godly life through our knowledge of him who called us by his own glory and goodness.

Dear friends,

Why is godly living so troubled, so harassed, so persecuted? Because godliness with contentment is great gain. In other words, if we want to live a godly life, and find peace, pleasure, happiness, contentment, we will bear much good fruit, which is a great gain. We will win souls. Which makes us a direct threat to the kingdom of darkness. The word content means that someone is satisfied. It is the state of sufficiency. If the devil can make us discontent, then God's grace is no longer sufficient. Once God's grace is no longer sufficient, the power of Christ no longer rests on us. Without the power of Christ, we become fruitless. No souls are won. God is not pleased. Checkmate, and we lose. We gain nothing, profit nothing, and become noise in the ears of God. Jesus said, apart from me we can do nothing. He is the all-sufficient one. Be content with that.

We are overcomers through the blood of the Lamb and our testimonies!

Titus 2:15 These, then, are the things you should teach. Encourage and rebuke with all authority. Do not let anyone despise you.

Dear friends,

What things are we supposed to teach? Teach things that go with sound doctrine, things that are in agreement with the entire word of God, things that accompany faith in God. Things that give us the power and strength to live a victorious life. Things that teach us discipline and righteousness. Things that make us more than conquerors through Christ who loves us. Teach things that overcome this world and things that we must pay close attention to and pray about continually. So, we may be worthy to escape all that is coming. Things, so that, we can stand before the Son of Man. Things that will transform us into the pure, clean, and spotless bride that Jesus is coming for quickly. Things that we do while we wait for the great and glorious appearing of the Lord. If anyone has a problem with it, they need to take it up with God. I am only a messenger.

1 Peter 4:13 But rejoice inasmuch as you participate in the sufferings of Christ, so that you may be overjoyed when his glory is revealed.

Dear friends,

I just remembered some of the trials God has brought me through. How every time I felt like I was being marked by the enemy, God would remind me that it is no big deal, just a little snag. God was not sleeping or taking a nap. He was not caught off guard or taken by surprise. He's got our backs. Jesus said we are blessed when we go through these things. For great is our reward, eternal rewards, with great glory. The apostle Paul called these problems light and momentary and wrote that these present-day suffering are not worthy of being compared, with the glory that will be revealed. James said, to count it all joy when we face trials so that we may be mature, complete, and not lacking anything. Peter wrote, give God glory, for the Spirit of Christ rests on us. So, when we go through these things. Remember this, to stay focused, and trust the Lord. Because we are not getting stuck. We are just going through.

Matthew 7:7 "Ask and it will be given to you; seek and you will find; knock and the door will be opened to you.

Dear friends,

Jesus told us to look for clues in answer to prayers. To ask, seek, and knock. These clues are found by seeking God. God has revealed Himself in His word. Every time we read God's word, we discover more clues. After we have gathered these clues, they become evidence. Evidence becomes a solid conviction of things not seen. Things that we have hoped for and prayed for. Then we can throw the book at the accuser. So, let us continue this search for clues. Also remember, to share the evidence.

7

1 Thessalonians 5:4 But you, brothers and sisters, are not in darkness so that this day should surprise you like a thief.

Dear friends,

So that day does not come on us suddenly like a trap. Since we all know that day will come like a thief in the night. Take caution to stay out of the darkness. Have nothing to do with its fruitless deeds, but rather expose them. When do most people sleep? When do people get drunk? In the morning or at night? Well, since we belong to the daylight let us be sober-minded, serious about our commitment to Jesus Christ. Walk in faith, hope, and love. For when perfection comes, all imperfection, or bad fruit will be burned up. Only three will remain. Faith, hope, and love. These are the remaining factors.

Romans 2:21 you, then, who teach others, do you not teach yourself? You who preach against stealing, do you steal?

Dear friends,

One of the things people do on Halloween is to put on a mask, and pretend they are something they are not. Paul makes it clear. He lays it out real plain and simple. Do people practice what they preach? One of the biggest disguises that a person can masquerade in is that of a hypocrite. A hypocrite is someone who says one thing and does another. A hypocrite does the very things that they condemn. One cannot avoid the truth by living a lie, and one cannot live a lie to avoid the truth. Take off the mask and live for Jesus. He loves us just the way we are.

1 John 1:9 If we confess our sins, he is faithful and just and will forgive us our sins and purify us from all unrighteousness.

Dear friends,

When I was a kid, I like to play baseball. I liked the game so much; I would often throw my baseball in the house. My father clearly warned me not to do this. He said, "things would get broken, and he would be very angry." Still, I did not listen, and I broke a window. When my dad saw it, he was angry. He said, "he told me not to play ball in the house," and was ready to punish me for disobeying. I was so scared and started crying. I said, "I know I'm not supposed to play ball in the house and I did not listen." Then I said, "I am so sorry dad, I should have listened. I will clean up the mess and pay for the window. Please forgive me." My dad was not angry anymore. He said he would clean up the mess. He did not want me to get cut. Then I asked him, "how much the window would cost." He said, "it was more than I had and he would pay." Jesus has paid for our sins and will clean up our mess. That's amazing love.

Genesis 4:7 If you do what is right, will you not be accepted? But if you do not do what is right, sin is crouching at your door; it desires to have you, but you must rule over it."

Dear friends,

When I was eight years old, I began playing little league baseball. My first year, I was placed in right field. There was one problem though. I did not know how to catch a fly ball. Well, my parents owned a tall farmhouse. I spent hours throwing my baseball on the roof at home. Then, I would catch the ball, as it rolled off. One day my dad saw what I was doing. He told me to stop before I broke another window. Again, I thought I had control, and disobeyed my father. I broke another window. I was so scared and hid the damage and avoided my father for almost a year. When he finally noticed the window gone, I denied any involvement. The damage was exposed, but I continued to avoid my father. I was controlled by fear because of my disobedience to my father. Sin had become my master. If only I had confessed, exposed the sin, and let my father deal with me.

J

John 10:3 The gatekeeper opens the gate for him, and the sheep listen to his voice. He calls his own sheep by name and leads them out.

Dear friends,

In a sporting game like football, basketball, or hockey the referee will regulate the game. His job is to declare the rules. He maintains the guidelines of the action. He is a kind of a watchman over the field. He does not make the plays. He just sees that the plays are run orderly. He will do this by blowing a whistle. Sometimes he blows the whistle, and it means time out. He did not call the time out. It was the team captain that made this call. The ref simply blows the whistle, as if he is opening a gate, for the captain to speak to the team. It is the captain who leads the team to victory. Well, Jesus is our captain. The victory belongs to Him.

Ephesians 5:10 And find out what pleases the Lord.

Dear friends,

When a referee blows the whistle it means time out, stop all action, pause the game. Now, some of the players will waste that time out. They will strut around boasting and bragging about how well they play. About how great they are for the team. About how they are going to win this one. Other players, will humble themselves. They think about their mistakes, and ways that they can improve in the game. Then, when they go back out, they do well. The players that do even better humble themselves, and then go to the coach. Because they want to know what he's thinking. What is going on in his mind? What does he want them to do differently? So important, what are his plans for the team? Time out.

Psalm 91:1 Whoever dwells in the shelter of the Most High will rest in the shadow of the Almighty.

Dear friends,

There is a secret place, a place of protection, where evidently, the enemy is powerless to touch us. Let the redeemed of the Lord say so. It is the place of rescue and escape. This is the place of God's grace. God's great grace! That means we do not deserve it, and there is nothing we can do to earn it. It is a gift of God. Simply because we love Him and acknowledge His Name. The Name of Jesus. It is the place of salvation. Eternal security. That means the protection of the eternal part of a person. Does this protection include our physical body? Sure, but this physical body will never become eternal. In other words, this physical body will pass away. Still, we are protected, and no harm will befall us, no disaster will come near. We will still have troubles, but our rescue, is imminent, in the works, and ready to happen. And when it comes, our rescue, our future glory will make those troubles seem trivial.

Philippians 3:15 All of us, then, who are mature should take such a view of things. And if on some point you think differently, that too God will make clear to you.

Dear friends,

Our assignment, should we choose to accept it. Is to grow in the knowledge of Christ through faith in Him. There is a wealth of knowledge to be discovered. Quite frankly it is a supreme advantage, a priceless privilege, with surpassing greatness to discover it. That's right; this is privileged information. Also, to whom much is given, much is required. These secrets are secured in Christ Jesus, through whom all the treasures of wisdom and knowledge are hidden. Know this; perfect revelation can be obtained by knowing Him actively, progressively, and fully. I don't claim to be perfect, but I will certainly press on in this investigation. My advice, to all who have ears to hear, do the same.

1 Corinthians 13:2 I have the gift of prophecy and can fathom all mysteries and all knowledge, and if I have a faith that can move mountains, but do not have love, I am nothing.

Dear friends,

The mystery of godliness is great. We can solve parts of it, and sadly, still, miss the big picture, come up short, gain nothing. Every great artist, musician, the chef has a trademark, signature, a secret ingredient. Something that says, this is their work. If that thing is missing it becomes a fake, a phony, incomplete, and worth nothing. The artist would say, that's not my signature. That's a forgery. The musician would say, that's not my song. I didn't write that. A master chef would say, that's not my cooking. This is missing my secret ingredient. Well, love is of God. love is God's trademark and signature, If love is missing, we are missing the key ingredient. It is what makes anything truly of God. I'm not talking about a worldly kind of love. I'm talking about a pure, holy, sacrificial kind of love. Every one that loves is born of God and knows God. For God is love. Listen, whatever we do, we must add Love.

1 Timothy 3:16 - Beyond all question, the mystery from which true godliness springs is great: He appeared in the flesh, was vindicated by the Spirit, was seen by angels, was preached among the nations, was believed on in the world, was taken up in glory.

Dear friends,

The mystery of godliness is great. Like all great mysteries, one needs to uncover it. It's not common knowledge. It is something a person is going to have to search for with all of their heart. I'm talking about true godliness. Some people have a form of godliness, but they deny its power. Have nothing to do with such people. See, Jesus is the power behind true godliness. He appeared in the flesh, was vindicated by the Spirit, was seen by angels, was preached among the nations, was believed on in the world, was taken up in glory. Yes, this mystery is great, but we can discover it.

1 Timothy 3:16 - Beyond all question, the mystery from which true godliness springs is great: He appeared in the flesh, was vindicated by the Spirit, was seen by angels, was preached among the nations, was believed on in the world, was taken up in glory.

Dear friends,

I have examined the facts, and I think this mystery is solved. True godliness Is not simply based on what we say or do? Or what we do not say and do not do. Is it not simply the ability to resist the devil, or say no to ungodliness True godliness is not simply living a self-controlled life? Dotting all the I's and crossing all the t's. It is not simply built on one's outstanding reputation or moral character? True godliness is not when someone says, he was a righteous man, or she was a virtuous woman. Therefore, I conclude that true godliness does not come from us at all, but springs from Jesus, the hope of glory.

1 Corinthians 3:18 - Do not deceive yourselves. If any of you think you are wise by the standards of this age, you should become "fools" so that you may become wise.

Dear friends,

Sometimes when we let God's plan unfold in our lives, it may seem impractical, unreasonable, even foolish. That's because in the natural. It is something that will make someone look undignified until it has God's signature on it. Often our flesh is going to say, no, don't do that, people are going to laugh. They might even say, that's crazy. Look at Noah, God told Noah to build an ark, and said, "the world is going to be flooded." Unheard of! God told Moses to approach Pharaoh and tell him to let my people go. Unthinkable! God told Mary she was pregnant with the savior of the world. Unprecedented! God told the disciples to take this gospel to the ends of the world. Unimaginable! Listen, if God is truly saying do it, He will also put His Name on it. In other words, He will endorsement it. By having His endorsement, it means no worry, fear, or stress. So, whatever we do, do it for the glory of God and when we hear his voice, be humble in the sight of the Lord. He will endorse that.

Colossians 3:4 When Christ, who is your life, appears, then you also will appear with him in glory.

Dear friends,

Colossians 3 tells us, to set our hearts and minds on things above, not the things of the Earth. For the world and the things of this world will pass away. It is the one who does the will of God that lives forever. Sure, in this world we will have troubles. Understand, that these present-day sufferings are not even worth comparing with the glory that will be revealed in us. So, remove, and eliminate the parts of life that are worldly. Live for Christ. Store up and gather eternal things. The things of God, things that will last forever. Put them away in heaven where Jesus Christ is seated in glory.

Hebrews 10:36 You need to persevere so that when you have done the will of God, you will receive what he has promised.

Dear friends,

Let's talk about the promises of God. The guaranteed words and spoken assurances of the Almighty. It is impossible for God to lie. He's not going to do it. It goes against the very makeup, the very character, which makes Him God. Let us hold on to those promises and kick it up another notch. Take it to a higher level. Being transformed from glory to glory. Crafted into the magnificence of Jesus Christ, through whom all God's promises are sure. They are yes, and amen. The best is yet to come. The Bible tells us of the good things God has done in the past. The wonders He performed. Know this; it gets even better. I know it sounds like a fortune cookie, but that's just the way God operates. He rolls like that. He saves the best for last! So, we're pressing on and growing strong. We are not giving up. For we believe God for a miraculous win!

2 Peter 1:10 Therefore, my brothers and sisters make every effort to confirm your calling and election. For if you do these things, you will never stumble,

Dear friends,

To each person who has received the call. We have seen the need, and we feel compelled to do something. How are we going to overcome the world? Well, do not fear for Jesus has already overcome the world. He has elected each person here to run this election and win this campaign. The campaign trail starts with faith in Jesus Christ. Add to faith goodness; and to goodness, knowledge; to knowledge, self-control; and to self-control, perseverance; to perseverance, godliness; and to godliness, mutual affection; to mutual affection, add love. Run this trail with an increasing measure. In other words, more and more. Not more or less, not less or less. So that each person's calling and election are sure. For we are standing on the promises of God. Take that to the bank.

Luke 21:34 Be careful, or your hearts will be weighed down with carousing, drunkenness and the anxieties of life, and that day will close on you suddenly like a trap.

Dear friends,

Be careful, or our hearts will get weighed down. Could it be any more obvious? This is a call to vigilance. To be cautiously aware of the sin all around, and the danger it presents. It may look harmless; it might hold promise or benefits. It might meet some real, or practical need. Quite frankly, it's a danger, a threat, and a trap. That's right; sin is the trap, not the day of the Lord. The day of the Lord brings salvation and restoration to those who are ready for it. Sin weighs us down and keeps us bound, but Jesus sets us free, and free indeed. Sin wants to rule over each person, but we must master it. Sin is looking for an opportunity, a foothold, a crack in the armor. So, it can choke the life out of us, but Jesus gives us life, and to the full. Say no to sin, make no room for the devil, resist him, and he will flee. Oh, and by the way, the devil is a liar, murderer, and thief. He is the source of all sin, for he has been sinning from the beginning. So be vigilant, be alertly and watchful, especially for the oncoming danger.

J

Matthew 25:5 The bridegroom was a long time in coming, and they all became drowsy and fell asleep.

Dear friends,

The virgins represent the church, which has been instructed to wait for Jesus to come again, at any moment. Well, the church waited and waited, and they all became tired in waiting. Sadly, they fell asleep. No one was watching. No one was expecting. It's like they all went in a cave waiting to be raptured. As prophecy is fulfilled, and the book of Revelation unfolds, God's people become sleepy. So, they are all taken by surprise. They are all caught off guard and unaware. They all knew their lover was coming and were burning to behold Him. Very sad, at some point, they lose that passion. Something causes them to sleep. Only some of them made it in before the door was shut. Before grace is no longer available. Jesus is telling us, He comes when no one expects Him. Not even His bride. Therefore, we must be vigilant, alertly, and watchful, for His coming. So, we do not fall victim to it.

2 Corinthians 6:14 Do not be yoked together with unbelievers. For what do righteousness and wickedness have in common? Or what fellowship can light have with darkness?

Dear friends,

God is about relationships! Often, the devil is unable to trick God's people into the obvious sin. Such as lying, stealing, or cursing. So, he will try to trap them in a relationship with someone in the world. It may be at work, school, church, etc. The most binding of these relationships is, without doubt, the marriage covenant. The apostle Paul cautions us not to tie a knot with an unbeliever. To tie a knot or become yoked is to make a bond that keeps people together. This bond or agreement could be as complex as a business deal or wedlock. It may also be as simple as a sporting event or lunch date. Therefore "Let him who stands, take caution, lest he falls." Relationships are a blessing when we build them God's way.

Isaiah 53:5 But he was pierced for our transgressions,

   he was crushed for our iniquities;

the punishment that brought us peace was on him,

   and by his wounds we are healed.

Dear friends,

   God is in the profession of healing. That is to say, that He is the pro!   Come on; we know it's true. Whether someone cuts their finger or stub a toe. Whether they are cured of cancer or some other life-threatening disease. Who is it that heals? Is it not him who can do exceedingly abundantly more than we can ask or think, according to the power that works in us? So, whose power is at work? God's power is at work through God's Holy Spirit. Yes, we know that we are the temple of God, and His Spirit lives in us, So, if the Spirit of the Great Physician lives in us, then that is something to rejoice over. The Healers in this house! Now get ready for exceedingly abundantly more!

1 Corinthians 9:24 Do you not know that in a race all the runners run, but only one gets the prize? Run in such a way as to get the prize.

Dear friends,

We must remember that we are in competition, and the prize is literally "out of this world"! We are not in competition with each other, but with everything that exalts itself against Christ. This means that we must spend time in training with our trainer, God's Spirit. Jesus went to the Father, but He did not leave us alone. He sent His own Spirit to dwell in us, so we too may overcome this world. We all have a time that we try to spend in His presence, in training, but the best competitors train all day long and dream about running in their asleep. The best runners also like to lose as many extra pounds as they can while in training, even if that means saying no to their favorite dessert. We must set aside the weight of sin and expose the deeds of darkness. It sounds like a lot of discipline, and I will not lie, it is. Let us remember the great cloud of witnesses that have run before us. None so perfect as our Lord, yet each has received a great reward.

John 2:8 "Whatever He says, do it"

Dear friends,

Some people call me the whistling prophet. This is because I am known to blow a sports whistle in church. This is something I have done since the 1990s. From the day of my conversion, I always had a heart filled with praise for the Lord. The church I attended was in renewal. When I decided to get in the river, I jump head first. Since I was already a worshiper, I felt like getting louder for God. Well, my voice could not reach the decibels that my heart contained. So., I bought a sports whistle. I'll never forget the fear I had first to blow that thing, but when the praises of God welled up in me, I exploded. It was like my lungs gave a glorious shout unto the Lord. Instantly the chains were broke, and all fear was gone. Since then I have learned that a whistles high pitch scream is more common as a warning signal. This has been effective in calling God's people to action and response. As I continue to obey God's call to blow a humiliating whistle, He continues to multiply the fruit it produces.

Psalm 62: 1 Truly my soul finds rest in God;

my salvation comes from him.

Dear friends,

When life is being ripped out from under us, we want to grab and hold on for dear life. Remember this, that the testing of our faith develops perseverance. Sometimes, to pursue one thing, we must let go of other wanted prizes. The greater the dedication to the pursuit, the lesser value given to things given up. Sometimes the pursuit becomes so hot that everything along the way becomes vague impressions. Let's turn our eyes upon Jesus, and the things of this world become strangely dim. Be very careful not to become careless with life, but to cast those cares, those concerns, and worries on that Rock.

Hebrews 6:19 We have this hope as an anchor for the soul, firm and secure. It enters the inner sanctuary behind the curtain,

Dear friends,

Ever seen the show "Let's Make A Deal"? I used to watch that show all the time when I was a kid. I was never too spiritual as a child, but I always had a desire to go for what was behind the curtain. The better that box prize looked, the more I would want the curtain. The devil wants us to keep the box. Some of us see worthless trash in the box. Others see the treasure. Some of us have become so comfortable with the box because it's what we see and know. As for me, I want the curtain. Be encouraged by these words today, the curtain is split, and Christ has entered in. This hope does not disappoint!

Proverbs 3:3 Let love and faithfulness never leave you; bind them around your neck, write them on the tablet of your heart.

Dear friends,

There is nothing I want more than God's favor. The favor of a man is nice to have, but even when men despise me God's favor blesses me. Love is supreme, for God is love, and if we truly love God, we will obey His commands. That means that we are faithful to His instructions, even when we don't understand, or agree with them. What's more is we do this with gladness, and His command is not burdensome. So, if my attitude is that "I'll do it, but I'm not going to like it," I'm going to miss God's favor. We can't rack up points for faithfulness and be lacking in love. Without love, it profits us nothing. To have faithfulness is to have a fullness of faith. Galatians 5:6 "The only thing that counts is faith expressing itself through love."

1 Corinthians 6:20 You were bought at a price.
Therefore, honor God with your bodies.

Dear friends,

Listen to a story about a man named Edward who loved dogs. He willingly paid a hefty price for his prize-winning Golden Retriever. He named his dog Beloved. Beloved would win every dog show he entered her in. Beloved was well known by the dog catcher for her roaming ways. Again, and again Edward had to pay the dog catcher so he could keep his beloved. Well, Beloved continued her roaming ways, and one-day Beloved got seriously hurt. Oh, Edward still cherished the mangled pup but poor Beloved's dog show days were over. If only Beloved would have honored her master. I'm not just talking to the dogs. We too must honor the Master with our bodies, so we can win the prize and bring Him glory.

Romans 7:25 Thanks be to God, who delivers me through Jesus Christ our Lord!

Dear friends,

Remember the man named Edward and his prize-winning dog, Beloved. Beloved would win all the dog shows. When Beloved got hurt, her dog show days were over. I too was hurt during my dog show days. I got in a serious car accident and was permanently marked with a disability. Sadly, that ended my dog show days. I think that we all have been hurt in one way or another. But our dog show days don't have to end badly. Receive Christ Jesus as Lord and Savior and the show has just begun. Access to far greater glory is given to us. The former show will seem like garbage once you taste and see that the Lord is good.

2 Corinthians 5:11 Since, then, we know what it is to fear the Lord, we try to persuade others. What we are is plain to God, and I hope it is also plain to your conscience.

Dear friends,

People will stand in lines and pay money to enter a haunted house and be scared stiff rather than seek the Lord and be scared straight. The world is wide awake to the fear of what some monster can do but asleep to God's authority. Does a child fear His father's authority? Certainly, a well-behaved child does. Not with a frightening fear but a respectful or reverential fear. It is the fear of the Lord that will influence us to think soberly. To live a self- controlled life and to have our heads on straight. For those who fear the Lord, He instructs them in holiness. Pay the most careful attention to Him. Stand in awe of who God is. He's great, mighty, and awesome.

Romans 8:2 For the law of the Spirit of life in Christ Jesus has set you free from the law of sin and of death.

Dear friends,

This is a true story about a horrible monster. Its name is sin. Sin desires to have us and to capture us. Sin wants to rule over us. Sin wants to be our master. So that we do its bidding and its evil deeds. So that we do things that are too shameful to even mention. After the transgression is completed, sin leaves us there to face the consequences. Sin also has a partner. Its name is death. Sin does the work then death collects the pay. So, God gave us laws to identify this monster but if we break these laws, even one, the monster shows we are guilty. So, the monster used these laws to increase its terror, by making sin utterly evil and we were trapped. Sin and death could then reign. Then God sent His Son, Jesus, who conquered sin and death. Jesus took their accusations and nailed them to the cross. He wiped out our guilt. He removed their power and authority. Making a public spectacle of them. He triumphed on our behalf.

It's winning grace,

winning grace,

winning grace!

Matthew 21:19 Seeing a fig tree by the road, he went up to it but found nothing on it except leaves. Then he said to it, "May you never bear fruit again!" Immediately the tree withered.

Dear friends,

There are several occurrences when Jesus is so displeased that He rebukes someone or something other than the devil. There is the time that the disciples stopped the children from coming to Him. The time Peter opened his mouth wrong. The time the money changers were selling in the temple. These are some prime examples. Here we find His rebuke has condemned this fig trees life. An absolute and final rebuke of judgment was pronounced. What motivated the Lord? It was the fact that this tree displeased Him. Find out what pleases the Lord and have nothing to do with the fruitless deeds of darkness. Quite frankly, if we want to please the Lord, we must bear good fruit.

Romans 1:20 For since the creation of the world God's invisible qualities—his eternal power and divine nature—have been clearly seen, being understood from what has been made, so that people are without excuse.

Dear friends,

There is something heavenly about creating something new. It gives me a sense of accomplishment to get those wheels turning and make the thing I pictured in my mind. One of the things I enjoy doing is creative cooking. I'll just take a little bit of this and mix it into that. Maybe add just a pinch of something else and bake it at 425 for 20 minutes and voilà! Perfecto! I believe that God gives each person some creative ability so we can all relate to His love for creation. God saw all that he had made, and it was very good. There was evening, and there was morning. Listen, God has invested in each person. He saw enormous potential and said it is very good. So be creative and use the gifts and the talents God has given and bring Him glory. Show the return to God on His investment.

2 Peter 3:9 The Lord is not slow in keeping his promise, as some understand slowness. Instead he is patient with you, not wanting anyone to perish, but everyone to come to repentance.

Dear friends,

What is it about waiting on God? We miss God's best when we don't wait and then we blame God for not moving fast enough. Now listen, if we can just learn to wait on the Lord, He will always show up and leave us speechless with amazement and wonder. With mind-blowing, eye-popping, jaw dropping bewilderment. For nothing is too difficult for God and with God all things are possible. We just need to embrace His timing. His timing is perfect. We may not ever understand it, because our world is so time-based, but a day is as a thousand years when suddenly He appears. He is King of kings and Lord of Lords. Trust Him; He's not going to drop the ball. Can we all just try to wait on the Lord?

Matthew 24:36 "But about that day or hour no one knows, not even the angels in heaven, nor the Son, but only the Father.

Dear friends,

The information is confidential. He's concealed that day until the appointed time. It's not even on a need to know basis. One would think the church would need to know. Right! God has us preparing and declaring that Jesus is coming but no mention of when. Or what about the angels that are ushering Jesus in. I can say this, that not even Jesus knows and He's the main event. Talk about confidential. The day is kept secret for means of revelation. For the mystery of God will be revealed and no one will be able to debate what every eye shall behold. When He comes, it will take the whole world by surprise, Like a thief in the night. For those who are eagerly awaiting His arrival, it will be salvation and eternal life. Look, I'm not a date setter, but this is a warning to be prepared. Let us not suppose that He is delaying or think that He is not coming at all. Let us not become so busy with life and weighed down by this world. Let us be awake and have nothing to hide. Let's make His coming to our blessed hope.

1 Peter 4:12 Dear friends, do not be surprised at the fiery ordeal that has come on you to test you, as though something strange were happening to you.

Dear friends,

Sometimes God will test our faith. He wants to see the evidence that we have confidence in Him and His promises. This will take patience and perseverance because it does mean that there will be some unwelcome surprises. Surprises that make us wonder what's going on here? Surprises that may even make us angry with God. Why now God? I will say this, Jesus had all these emotions, yet He still chose to endure the cross because God so loved the world. Jesus gave His life for us. He was obedient even unto death. The best part is that He rose again to confirm the promise. The promise is eternal life for all who believe.

1 Timothy 4:8 For physical training is of some value, but godliness has value for all things, holding promise for both the present life and the life to come.

Dear friends,

Let us prepare for today's workout by stretching. Let us stretch our faith. This means to dream big! Think outside the box. Envision that thing that could never happen unless God gets involved. Now trust God as we reach for that thing. God can do far more than we could ever ask for or imagine. Now let's get right into cardiovascular and start running after God. Set those hearts on things above. Treasure eternal things. For where our treasure is our hearts will be. Be enthusiastic and exercise those gifts. Ok, now let's take some time and just rest in His presence. Feel that release. Breathe in the Holy Spirit. Let all the worries and the troubles of this life fade away. The things of this Earth grow dim, as we focus on Him. Take time to just marvel and wonder at Him. He has done and will continue to do great things in and through us. Now give God the glory through Jesus. Amen!

2 Peter 2:19 They promise them freedom, while they themselves are slaves of depravity—for "people are slaves to whatever has mastered them.

Dear friends,

Are we enjoying this glorious freedom that Christ has given us? Well good, but listen, because this is very important, we can ruin this glorious freedom if we allow wicked minds to control us. I will say it again; if we let crooked influences have power in our world, then we can kiss this great liberty goodbye. Sadly, we will end up with corrupt policies again. Possibly even seven times worse than before. Therefore, ask the Holy Spirit to fill our house with men and women of good character. Because quite frankly, a good character will continue to make God's Kingdom great here on the earth.

J

*1 Peter 3:15 But in your hearts revere Christ as Lord.
Always be prepared to give an answer to everyone
who asks you to give the reason for the hope that you
have. But do this with gentleness and respect,*

Dear friends,

Ever noticed the reaction of a little child who
knows the answer to a question? They become
overjoyed with excitement to share the information
they know. Their faces will light up with a smile, as
they raise their hand and wave it in the air. When the
teacher calls on them, they are ready to give an
answer. We should have the same passion for sharing
our knowledge of Jesus. Because we know the
answer! We need to do this properly so that they
listen to our answer. If the child is wild and burst out
yelling "pick me, pick me, pick me" no one will listen. If
the child is rude or disrespectful and forcefully blurts
out the answer. They are often ignored and passed
over. See It's important that we are excited about
Jesus and prepared to witness in word and speech.
But quite frankly, the only way it will ever be effective
is if we are sensitive to His Spirit and revere Christ as
Lord in our hearts.

Psalm 46:10 He says, "Be still, and know that I am God; I will be exalted among the nations, I will be exalted in the earth."

Dear friends,

These Newly-weds were driving across the country for a vacation. The man had every minute planned and was on a strict schedule. Well, the man stopped for gas but did not awaken his wife. When he went inside to pay the wife woke up and got out of the car to use the restroom. Then he came back out, jumped in the car, assuming that his wife was still asleep in the back, he took off. About an hour later a policeman pulled him over. When the officer approached his car, the man said, "What seems to the problem officer, I know I wasn't speeding?" The policeman said, "Are you all alone?" The man said, "No, my wife is asleep in the back." My point is this; when life gets busy, it's easy to move on without the Lord and leave His presence. Be still and know.

Psalm 84:10 Better is one day in your courts than a thousand elsewhere; I would rather be a doorkeeper in the house of my God than dwell in the tents of the wicked.

Dear friends,

Heaven's doorkeeper. Does that sound like heaven? Maybe not, but the writer is not really talking about heaven. He's talking about serving God right here on earth just to spend time in His presence. He's willing to work the lowest and most humbling position for just a glimpse of the master. It does not matter what God wants him to do as long as they are together. He has made the Lord his firm foundation, and he knows he cannot be shaken as long as he remains in God's presence. We need to be ready to do the will of God. To give everything up just to follow Jesus. Just to experience the blessedness of being God's chosen instrument. Even if it means the lowest position? Mopping floors, mowing grass, or taking out the garbage. Think about it.

Isaiah 55:9 "As the heavens are higher than the earth,

so are my ways higher than your ways

and my thoughts than your thoughts."

Dear friends,

Ever try to solve a puzzle without all the pieces there? It is impossible unless the missing pieces are found. It boggles the mind trying to fit pieces together. Something is puzzling about the mind of God. I have heard it said, that if we can grasp one of God's thoughts, it will change the world forever. Well, the puzzle was solved for us by Jesus Christ. For all the treasures of wisdom and knowledge are in Christ. Therefore, access to understanding is available to all who remain in Christ and walk in His Spirit. That's right, Christ holds the treasures and gives an all-access pass to these treasures, but the Spirit unlocks these treasures. Do we want to know the thoughts of God? Then we need to ask Christ to breathe on us and receive the Spirit. Then the puzzle is completed.

Roman 8:39 neither height nor depth, nor anything else in all creation, will be able to separate us from the love of God that is in Christ Jesus our Lord.

Dear friends,

There is one that sticks closer than a brother, and He says that nothing can separate us from His love. It is a love we cannot lose, and it will never be taken away from us. His love endures forever. It is described as better than life! There is nothing we can say or do to receive any more or less than all of His love, all of the time. His love is steady and unchanging. It will blow our minds trying to understand it. It's just that thorough, all-inclusive. It's unfathomable. What might love like this cost? One hundred dollars, one thousand dollars, one million dollars? How about nothing? That's right; it won't cost a thing. It's already been paid for by Jesus Christ. All we have to do is open our heart and receive it. Think of it as a birthday present. For the moment one receives this gift of love, they are born again.

Philippians 1:12 Now I want you to know, brothers and sisters, that what has happened to me has actually served to advance the gospel.

Dear friends,

Heaven is in our hearts, but that doesn't mean everything is going to be heavenly. If we are going to grow, we are going to have to stretch. If we are going to go deeper, we have to do some digging. If we are going to level up, we must first complete the level we are on. It is the same with God! We must stretch our faith, dig into His word, and complete His will. Well, stretching sounds painful, digging sounds like work, and leveling up sounds like a lot of time and commitment. I'm going to have to endure some things. Well, that's all true. But if we can do this, stretching we will grow, digging we will discover, and leveling up means advancement. It's a promotion. God will elevate us, but the more resistance, the more painful the ordeal.

1 Kings 17:21 Then he stretched himself out on the boy three times and cried out to the Lord, "Lord my God, let this boy's life return to him!"

Dear friends,

Someone who embraces calisthenics or aerobics has less resistance to stretching than someone who does no exercise. They can do straddles and splits with little resistance. When a less active person struggles to touch their knees. The less resistance a rubber band has, the farther it can stretch. We too must stretch our faith to break any resistance to God. That way our spirits are flexible and responsive when He wants to move us. So how do we stretch my faith? By exercising the gifts. By exercising our gifts, we become flexible to the move of God. For our spirits to become sensitive to God's Spirit. The word of God will strengthen our spirits, but it is not enough to simply know our bible. Even if we got the bible memorized from cover to cover, we must also do the word, or we are only tricking ourselves. This can be hard and quite frankly, uncomfortable at times but is vital to proper growth. Still, I have confidence and believe that we will not neglect our gift nor let it remain idle.

John 6:12 When they had all had enough to eat, he said to his disciples, "Gather the pieces that are left over. Let nothing be wasted."

Dear friends,

Jesus had just worked one of His great miracles. He had fed five thousand people with five loaves and two fish. Incredible! How many times has God done something incredible in our lives and we threw out the pieces? I'm talking about major spiritual breakthroughs. God does want us to set them aside, in the sense that we are no longer entangled in them. But Jesus did say "let nothing be wasted." Listen to what He said and don't waste the fragments. I know that they remind us of hard times. Times of lack, restlessness, weariness, doubt, and uncertainty. God may just be teaching us something. Therefore, gather these pieces to minister God's miracle in another person's life.

2 Corinthians 4:13 It is written: "I believed; therefore I have spoken. "Since we have that same spirit of faith, we also believe and therefore speak,

Dear friends,

We need to be vocal about the salvation that God has given to us in Jesus Christ. Let the joy of the Lord burst from our lips with thanksgiving. Remember, true life begins after we meet the Lord in the sky. After we share in His glorious resurrection. It is to our benefit, meaning we create great wealth by gratefully sharing this good news with other people. By doing this, more and more eyes are opened. More and more hearts are changed. More and more God's kingdom grows and so does our reward. It's a win/win to the glory of God.

2 Corinthians 3:5 Not that we are competent in ourselves to claim anything for ourselves, but our competence comes from God.

Dear friends,

It is very important that we recognize our dependence on God. We do not have the ability to change a heart apart from God. We need His signature. A signature that is not our own or any other persons but belongs to our Master. This signature is not on a paper, notepad, computer screen, or any other physical form. A signature that is, "not signed with ink but with the Spirit of God." This signature is worth much more than any human endorsement. Without this signature ministry becomes worthless. It becomes nothing more than a religious circus, which can be very entertaining but lacks any enduring substance. It may draw some attention in this life, but it's just hay, wood, and stubble when the smoke clears. That may work for some, but let's seek gold, silver, and precious gems, the things that God will sign for. Then, when the price tag is beyond our line of credit, we have His signature.

J

Hebrews 11:2 This is what the ancients were commended for.

Dear friends,

The ancients were commended by God for their faith. Does that statement apply to the people living today? Certainly not the world in general but what about the church? I'd like to think that our faith is pleasing God but, if we stop some paychecks, repossess some cars or houses, how sure and certain will our faith remain? If He strikes the shepherd will the sheep be scattered? Well, it happened to the disciples and they all fell. Still, God picked them up again. All, except the one who gave up and hung himself. I believe that God would have picked him up too if he would have endured for a time. Never Give up believing Jesus.

Proverbs 10:5 He who gathers crops in summer is a prudent son, but he who sleeps during harvest is a disgraceful son.

Dear friends,

      Thanksgiving is a time of rejoicing in God for the year's harvest. Now, the summer's over and the wise child of God has been gathering valuable crops all year long. It's wisdom in Jesus, wisdom in Jesus. Now, the wise child of God has been watching the signs of the times, and they can see what is coming. Or should I say who is coming? That's right; they are not unaware. They can see that day approaching, and they are awake. But many have been sleeping, and quite frankly, it's disgraceful. Wake up, wake up. For the end time harvest is near.

John 21:17 The third time he said to him, "Simon son of John, do you love me?"

Peter was hurt because Jesus asked him the third time, "Do you love me?" He said, "Lord, you know all things; you know that I love you."

Jesus said, "Feed my sheep."

Dear friends, did the Lord know that Peter loved Him? Yes, the Lord knows all things. That means He knew that Peter would be hurt when He asked Him three times. Jesus loves us too much to pull any punches, figuratively speaking. Sometimes we even need to be on the receiving end of a good spiritual sucker punch. That is to say, "I didn't even see it coming." Understand, God loves us too much to let us simply sweep our mistakes under the carpet. He is not going to embarrass us in front of the whole world, but He is going to expose those deeds of darkness so that our hearts are broken. It is in our brokenness that God can teach us. Peter had heard Jesus say that if he loved Him will do what I say, but now He heard loud and clear "Feed My Sheep."

Matthew 3:8 "Produce fruit in keeping with repentance."

Dear friends,

Sometimes children will do things they think really pleases daddy. It might be something that even puts a smile on father's face, but after a moment of reflection on the act, daddy is not so pleased. Then when dad gets angry, they claim that his instructions were not clear enough. Then dad has a choice. He can second guess his words, or he can take action. I am confident that with our Heavenly Father there is no second-guessing. He knows His word is clear and there is no double-mindedness. Maybe we made Him smile for a while, but then things went sour. Don't look for an out and try to find an excuse. That will only ensure judgment. Come clean and confess the disobedience. Because when a child repents with tears in their heart, daddy cannot help but forgive for his heart is broken. How much greater are His mercies and grace when repentance is genuine.

J

Philippians 4:19 And my God will meet all your needs according to the riches of his glory in Christ Jesus.

Dear friends,

Parents will prepare and serve breakfast, lunch, and dinner for their children. If the meal they serve is too small or missing something, the child may say "Is that all we get?" Suddenly the parent may feel an urgency to meet that need and they often ask my child what else they want. The parent may rifle through the cabinets, drawers, fridge, and sometimes they will even go to the store to meet that need. Whether the child has been good or bad does not even factor in when it is something that they need. Good or bad are considered when it's dessert time. That's when they are rewarded accordingly. Isn't it great to be a child of God!

James 1:2 Consider it pure joy, my brothers and sisters, whenever you face trials of many kinds,

Dear friends,

Sometimes we must feed our children something we know they won't like. We know there is going to be trouble getting them to eat it. But how pleased we are when they finish the plate without fuss. Think how pleased the heavenly Father must be when we willingly obey no matter how horrible the taste. I'm talking about doing it for Daddy. Simply to make him smile. God is honored when we choose to grin and bear it. Sometimes we may feel like there is more on our plate than we can handle. That may very well be the case. If we could handle the temptation, we would not need Him. This is no time to give up. Giving up now is not trusting God, who has made a way out. This is the time to seek God like never before joyfully.

2 Corinthians 2:7 Now instead, you ought to forgive and comfort him, so that he will not be overwhelmed by excessive sorrow.

Dear friends,

What is it within our human nature that makes a person have to prove they are right? Why do people have to continue beating each other over the head to prove their point? We all have been guilty of this. We have all had disagreements and let our tongues tear, cut, and slash to uphold our argument. Maybe our argument was the truth, but the devil's devices become our rebuttal. Now everyone's sad and hurt, including the Spirit, who is grieved. Do not try to bury this thing or sweep it under the carpet and think that time will heal all wounds. Forgive and comfort that person. What they did may have been wrong, but it is as if they never did it. Now comfort that person. Don't depend on time but trust God for the healing.

Matthew 6:21 For where your treasure is, there your heart will be also.

Dear friends,

If we can just set our hearts on things above, on the things surrounding Christ in glory. Then that is where our treasure will be. Then we will be rich toward God. Money, power, and position are here today and gone tomorrow. I'm sure we have all heard horror stories on that the United States currency is not worth the paper it is printed. That the American dollar is fake. It's just a matter of time before this bubble burst. It's not just the U.S. The Bible tells us that the world's economy is going to collapse. But I'm not trying to scare anyone with end time prophecy. I just want to point to something that will last. Eternal treasures.

Luke 12:51 Do you think I came to bring peace on earth? No, I tell you, but division.

Dear friends,

I love this scripture because to me it is very sobering. By sobering I mean it cleans out the poisons of this world that pollute our minds and keep us from seeing clearly. Yes, God can and will add and subtract things in our lives. He gives and takes away, blessed be the name of the Lord! We love it when He multiplies our blessings and our cups overflow, but the Lord's purpose in all these things is to divide or separate the sheep from the goats, the wheat from the weeds, Godly from ungodly, believer from the unbeliever. Only those who are on God's side of the dividing line will be saved from destruction. Be sober-minded.

Romans 8:28 And we know that in all things God works for the good of those who love him, who have been called according to his purpose.

Dear friends,

I can remember when I was a child and watching Sesame Street, Mr. Rogers, and The Electric Company. After this fabulous lineup, a program would come on called The Joy of Painting. It featured a gentle and calm artist by the name of Bob Ross. He would paint happy little trees and happy little rocks. Everything he painted was filled with happy little things. The best part was when he made a mistake; he would turn it into a happy little accident. He had this power because he was the artist and the canvas was his happy little world. Well, the world is God's happy little canvas. The world may seem less than happy because we try to control this world and break away from God's plan. This is a big mistake! When we walk in the love of God and give Him the control, He will turn those mistakes into happy little accidents. When He has completed the picture, it will be beautiful.

Mark 13:22 For false messiahs and false prophets will appear and perform signs and wonders to deceive, if possible, even the elect.

Dear friends,

Two people are traveling to the same destination. One reads the signs and follows their own leading. The other traveler reads the signs but is led by G.P.S. Ok, now imagine some deviant, some trickster, moves one of the road signs to cause confusion. They want to throw travelers off track. Which of the two do will recognize that false leading? Which of the two becomes obsessed with finding another sign? Pray that the Lord opens our eyes to interpret the signs. Do not blindly follow the signs; they can be misleading. Follow God who always leads us to glorious procession in Christ. Use God's G.P.S Glorious Procession System.

James 1:12 Blessed is the one who perseveres under trial because, having stood the test, that person will receive the crown of life that the Lord has promised to those who love him.

Dear friends,

When a TV station goes off the air at night sometimes color bars come on the screen often accompanied by a high-pitched tone. This means the station has gone to sleep. Sometimes, this will happen during the day. It may mean the station is having technical problems or it may simply be a test. If it is a test, the station will notify us. I remember the panic I felt, seeing the bars and hearing the tone, until the station would announce, "This is only a test." Well, God does not have technical problems, and He is always awake. So, when we have troubles in life take it to God. He is our help. Do not panic with fear. Be glad! If trouble continues, know that it is only a test. When the test is complete, regularly scheduled programming will continue, and the picture will be clear.

Mark 4:37 A furious squall came up, and the waves broke over the boat, so that it was nearly swamped.

Dear friends,

We all know the story well, and we know that Jesus calms the storm. His exceedingly great power and authority kept his people safe and amazed beyond natural comprehension. Nevertheless, when there is a storm, there is water damage. Often God makes us responsible for the drainage. He has sent His Holy Spirit to give us the strength, knowledge, equipment, and everything else needed to get the job done. It's a good thing to marvel at what God has done, but if we want to see more, we need to get the water out of the boat.

There is victory in Jesus who always leads in triumph!

Ephesians 5:16 Making the most of every opportunity, because the days are evil.

Dear friends,

Does this mean that we need to be occupied at the Lord's work? Does it mean that if we are not busy helping others, we are wasting all our time, for we are called to take on the role of a servant? I want to ask all of us to rethink the traditional interpretation of this verse. Because there is more, even better! Remember when Mary was not busy helping Martha serve Jesus. Martha got angry and felt Mary was wasting her time. Jesus told Martha that what Mary was doing was even better. Mary was not busy, and there was much work to be done. Still, she was commended for making the most of the opportunity. She rested to spend time and just listen to Jesus. "Well done good and faithful servant."

Philippians 1:18 "But what does it matter? The important thing is that in every way, whether from false motives or true, Christ is preached. And because of this I rejoice. Yes, and I will continue to rejoice,"

Dear friends,

When a child is given a chore to do usually it is going to require an incentive. Some type of bargaining chip. For example, mow the lawn, and I'll give twenty dollars. The lawn gets mowed. The father slips the child the bill. Everybody is happy. Nobody cares thatthe job was done out of false motives for no one knew about the incentive, nor did they see the exchange. But what about the child that does all the work for no other reason than to please dad? A selfish and lazy father will take advantage of that faithful child, but a good and loving father will reward that child openly and give him/her great honor. Our Heavenly Father is good and full of love.

Luke 10:42 "But few things are needed—or indeed only one. Mary has chosen what is better, and it will not be taken away from her."

Dear friends,

We have all sinned, made mistakes, have regretted. Hopefully, we have confessed those things to God, been forgiven, and set free. Then we rejoice in that freedom and become busy doing the work of the Kingdom. This is a good thing that we should bear good fruit. What if we choose to surrender that freedom to be near Him? "Draw near to God, and He will draw near to us." But I'm so busy; I have no time, my schedule is crazy. I know we all have responsibilities but let's make a relationship with God top priority. Fruit that last comes out of knowing Him intimately.

Philippians 3:12 Not that I have already obtained all this, or have already arrived at my goal, but I press on to take hold of that for which Christ Jesus took hold of me.

Dear friends,

Paul writes that all former things are a loss. This is easy to understand. Everyone agrees that the things done before conversion were meaningless. Like all money made, things bought, awards, certificates, trophies... Then Paul takes it even further and says, he counts all things loss. This includes things after conversion. Things like fruitfulness, good works, and eternal treasures. He has come to realize that even these things get in the way of him clearly perceiving Christ. Not that Paul would ever neglect these things, but they disadvantage him from fully knowing God. Think about it.

Luke 14:26 "If anyone comes to Me and does not hate his father and mother, wife and children, brothers and sisters, yes, and his own life also, he cannot be My disciple."

Dear friends,

This can be a very difficult verse to interpret. Why does Jesus use such a strong word as hate? Does He want us to leave the people who have been so supportive in our lives? Furthermore, we are told to hate our own lives. Surely Jesus is not teaching suicide. Could Jesus be saying that everything in life, including life itself, becomes an obstacle, a roadblock, and even handicaps us from following God? Preventing us from getting a better grasp on who He is and His plan for us? Do we love Jesus so much that we are ready to shut the door on everyone and everything that has been so meaningful to us? Just to hear what he's saying. This is the discipline and devotion of a disciple.

Luke 2:48 When his parents saw him, they were astonished. His mother said to him, "Son, why have you treated us like this? Your father and I have been anxiously searching for you."

Dear friends,

Did Jesus know the torture He was putting His parents through? Why did He not tell them He was going to remain in the temple? It is almost as if He hated them. Of course, we know this is not the case. We know that Jesus had a great love for His mother and Joseph. When they did find Him, He respectfully followed them and was obedient. He did make one comment, "I had to be about my Father's business." See Jesus was not causing heartache to His parents. He simply put pleasing His Father first. He knew that telling them would only be an obstacle. In the same way, He expects His followers to abandon anything that prevents them from pleasing God.

Luke 2:44 Thinking he was in their company, they traveled on for a day. Then they began looking for him among their relatives and friends.

Dear friends,

A father was out shopping with His son and took his eyes off his boy for a minute. He heard the boy mumble something but was not really listening. He turned around, and the boy was gone. Great panic came over the man. Where was his son? Well, many Christian are feeling that same panic today. They are waking up and saying "Where is Jesus" assuming He was on pause. We have been so busy doing our business and fail to notice. He moved on. He found his son after he searched for him with all his heart. He was looking at a video game and told dad he was going. My point is this. If we are only half listening and assuming the Lord is in our company we may end up in a panic.

Romans 16:25 Now to him who is able to establish you in accordance with my gospel, the message I proclaim about Jesus Christ, in keeping with the revelation of the mystery hidden for long ages past,

Dear friends,

He will establish us. He is able! To establish means to cause to be recognized and appoint permanently. God wants to do this in our lives, but we keep backing down. We are ok with persevering as long as things are good. Then things get a little tough, and we start sweating. So why are we so surprised when we miss this promise after we lose heart? Every time we grab on to some other means of comfort, we have lost heart. Stop grabbing on to people, places, things, positions, fantasies, and other temporal comforts. Let's make up our minds to be recognized in accordance with Christ even when that means sharing in His sufferings. Don't miss His next appointment!

Matthew 5:41 If someone forces you to go one mile, go two miles with him.

Dear friends,

A person may demand that we go a mile for them, and the bible rightly instructs that we go two. We are to give generously, ungrudgingly, without counting the cost. Many of us do this well when the demand is present, but the Holy Spirit is a gentleman. He will not force anyone to go a mile. He has advised us to seek the Lord and promised that we would find him when we seek him with all our heart and with all our soul. Jesus said to ask, seek, knock and attached similar promise. The promise has been made. We just need to go the mile without force. If someone has walked that mile, they know the promise is true! Now, what if? What if we go the extra mile?

Matthew 3:2 And saying, "Repent, for the kingdom of heaven has come near."

Dear friends,

One of the most admired qualities in this world is a great strength. Wrestling is a sport that awards strength. When wrestling with sin, the greatest strength is confronting our weakness. The longer we are dressed in the cover-up of pride and denial the longer we remain wrapped up in the sin, and remember, sin is death. The only cure is true repentance. This means more than simply a guilty conscience that causes someone to deeply regret the wrongdoing. Repentance involves the change of direction, walking away from the offense, and moving toward God. It's when one stops repenting that they stop moving toward God. Let me encourage everyone to be quick to repent. Do not let fears of the offense prevent this. Be on guard against greed, pride, and other things which also keep one from true repentance. God is loving, kind, and full of mercy. Walk humbly before our God!

1 Peter 2:3 Now that you have tasted that the Lord is good.

Dear friends,

A father bought his son a toy that required assembly. It looked like a really fun gadget, so he exhausted his efforts to put this gizmo together. He spent over an hour working on this thing so that his son would be thrilled with his dad. Well, when he was done, he called his son over to see it work. The father turned it on and was dazzled by what it did. Then he handed it over to his son, who was less than excited. When he was finished, he looked at his dad and said, "What now?". Dad's heart dropped as he said: "I guess that's it." Well, Peter tells us now what. He says now that we have tasted that the Lord is good, live a clean life. We must rid ourselves of all filth. Crave more of God, and He will provide. He will make us marvel in amazement. For what we have now is just a taste. "What now" is a child's response. Peter is instructing us how to grow in our salvation.

Psalm 94:18 When I said, "My foot is slipping,"

your unfailing love, Lord, supported me.

Dear friends,

Our enemy is real, and his craft and power are great. He is filled with cruel hate. On earth, there is no equal. Those are the lyrics to "A Mighty Fortress" and how true they are. One of the tactics of the devil is to keep people bound in shame. If he can make us feel low and unworthy, we remain trapped. We remain weak and unprotected because we are afraid to approach God. If we do gather the courage to approach Him, the shame still prevents us from coming clean. We are afraid that we will be rejected by a holy God. The truth is that if we can be honest and open with God, He is lovingly waiting. Tell Him "My foot is slipping." His love is not only waiting but will also support us. On earth, Satan has no equal, but A Mighty Fortress is our God, and He shall win the battle!

Luke 22:51 But Jesus answered, "No more of this!" And he touched the man's ear and healed him.

Dear friends,

Ever wonder, "How can this be the will of God? God would not want His people to suffer like this." We think as Peter, "They are trying to take away our Lord". So, our natural response is to fight. Fight the schools, fight the government, fight the doctors, ... I'm not saying there is anything wrong with taking a position based on our convictions and standing our ground. That is our duty. But when we are cutting off someone's ear, be it literally or figuratively, God is not pleased. He might even say "No more of this, stop it or enough. See Peter thought he was defending Jesus, but it was God's will that Jesus was taken away for a time. The true believer does not need to fight to hold on to their convictions. They just need to hold on to their convictions for the fight.

Matthew 20:40 Then he returned to his disciples and found them sleeping. "Couldn't you men keep watch with me for one hour?" he asked Peter.

Dear friends,

We do not want to fall asleep while waiting for the Lord. That's a pretty rough sleep. When one wakes up the enemy is trying to take away their Lord. The enemy is trying to snuff Him out of our minds whenever we wander off. Then all we can do is a retreat. Sometimes retreating is necessary to survive. If so, do not become a lazy dog. Spend time and strengthen that eager, ready for anything part of our being. When we feel strong, and the presence of the Lord has consumed us. When the glory of God is disbursed, and we think we are exploding from unspeakable joy and a peace we cannot understand! Stick it out. Ask the Lord if He will allow us to remain there a little while longer. Our minds are going to remind us of things that have to be done. Everything is going to seem important. My advice is just to remain and hold on.

Luke 23:23 "But with loud shouts they insistently demanded that he be crucified, and their shouts prevailed."

Dear friends,

Their shout for injustice prevailed. Jesus was an innocent man and willingly took the punishment of the cross. Why? Because God so loved the world that He sent Jesus, His one and only Son. That's right; it was God's love that sent His Son into this sinful world as a sacrifice for our sins. He endured beating, bruising, cuts, insults, mocking, thorns, nails, swords, whips ... He shed blood and was crucified. He took it all on out of love for us. So, love conquered death when He arose from the grave. The Love of God prevailed over the shouts for crucifixion. Let His love compel us every day.

John 6:37 *"All that the Father gives me will come to me, and whoever comes to me I will never drive away."*

Dear friends,

Is this talking about salvation? Yes! But this is so much more than the moment of conversion. It is the continual coming to Christ. The working of our salvation for faith takes work. It is the work of believing and that takes action. It is spending time with the Boss. Like any job sometimes it's easy or fun, a joy to do. Some people say that they would do their job for nothing. The paycheck is just a bonus. Other people say work is less fun and have to push themselves to do it. They can think of a million other things they want to do. Nevertheless, they continue to work to sustain life. In this passage, Jesus tells us that He is the bread of life. Salvation is the free gift of God which is through faith. Faith requires work. Jesus has done the work. Therefore, we need to be constantly coming and feeding off Him, "The bread of life" to sustain life. When someone discovers this Jesus will never drive them away.

Luke 1:52 He has brought down rulers from their thrones

but has lifted up the humble.

Dear friends,

How low can we go? I'm not talking about politics, acts of transgression, dating choices, or dancing under the limbo stick. I'm talking about humbling ourselves. One of the hardest things to do is to take on the role of a servant and consider our own wants and desires unworthy of being met. Let us not forget that Jesus did this very thing when He put on human skin, walked on this earth, and died on the cross. He told the Father that this suffering was not what He wanted but remained humble. He went as low as one can go. He descended to the gates of hell. Therefore, God exalted Him. He lifted Him. Will we humble ourselves and serve our Savior? Please understand, the lower we humble ourselves, the higher He lifts us.

Proverbs 24:16 For though the righteous fall seven times, they rise again, but the wicked stumble when calamity strikes.

Dear friends,

God has called us out of the darkness and makes us shine. Will we still be tempted? Absolutely! Possibly even worse than those who are enslaved to sin? Sometimes people fall back into some of those old behaviors, and they feel as though they are in bondage again. They dare not tell anyone for reasons of shame and fear. Been there done that. Rise up, oh child of God. The Father loves you. I am not trying to excuse anyone's wrongdoing. The good news is we can escape. This trip does not have to end in disaster. Return to God and rise up again!

Luke 13:8 "'Sir,' the man replied, 'leave it alone for one more year, and I'll dig around it and fertilize it.

Dear friends,

A lesson from the claw. That game in grocery stores, discount stores, and pizza restaurants. That game that grabs prizes and drops them out for the kids. Kids get so excited every time they see one. They hope that it will produce what they desire. If the claw returns without anything, they are greatly disappointed. The more they invest in the claw, the more they expect. But when the machine comes up empty, they still see potential. God is well pleased when we produce good fruit and desires that we produce much. God expects us to produce by what He gave us. When we come up empty, we might feel useless, but God sees the potential.

Psalm 30:5 For his anger lasts only a moment,

but his favor lasts a lifetime;

weeping may stay for the night,

but rejoicing comes in the morning.

Dear friends,

Who like happy endings? All the pain and suffering become trivial. Life is not easy when we choose to follow God. The way is hard, and we will undoubtedly make some messes. God already knows this and has a plan to rescue us. He will never abandon His children. No mess that we make is too big for our God. This does not remove the seriousness of the offense. God will never smile at our sins. If a person makes a mess, they need to clean it up. What happens when a person ignores the mess or try to cover it up? Eventually, it will be exposed. They must face the mess and confess their faults and failings to God, His mercy, grace, forgiveness, and love are great. Troubles may come but for a moment. Happily, ever after means forever and is not just a fairy tale.

Luke 2:19 But Mary treasured up all these things and pondered them in her heart.

Dear friends,

Mary treasured the things that the shepherds told her in her heart. She not only treasured these things but also pondered them. By pondering such things, she made sure that her treasure was being stored up in heaven. For when we think on these things, God guards our hearts and minds in Christ Jesus. Mary pondered the good news the shepherds brought her. The good news about the baby being the Christ, the Messiah, Lord of all, and Savior of the world. The good news that amazed all who heard it. Yes, Mary treasured the Good News in her heart and made a good deposit in heaven.

Psalm 111:2 Great are the works of the Lord;

they are pondered by all who delight in them.

Dear friends,

Just take a moment and ponder the miracle of Christmas. Consider the miracle of the Savior of the world, the Messiah, the Lord whose works are great, appearing as a newborn baby in a manger. He offers salvation to all who believe by way of the cross. He laid down His greatness to dwell with us. He is Immanuel, God with us. It's good news with great joy for everybody that God's favor rests on the earth, bringing peace and goodwill to all men and women. Let's not forget about the women. For in Christ Jesus, there is no inequality.

Luke 10:40 But Martha was distracted by all the preparations that had to be made. She came to him and asked, "Lord, don't you care that my sister has left me to do the work by myself? Tell her to help me!"

Dear friends,

One night a father put the wet clothes in the dryer and turned it on. Then he went to read devotions to his kids. Well, the buzzer went off on the dryer, and his youngest son ran to get the clothes. When he came back, he was mad that his older brother did not help him. He complained to dad and told him to tell the brother to get up and help him. He did not comply with his wishes though, not because he did not care about his struggle, but because he was pleased that his older son was clinging to Jesus. He was not going to take that away from Him, and God will never take that away from His children.

2 Corinthians 8:7b . . . - see that you also excel in this grace of giving.

Dear friends,

Are we cheerful givers? Does it bring us happiness, joy, and delight to present our best gift? See, it's not the amount or magnificence of the gift that matters to God. It's the heart and attitude in which the gift is given. Whatever the circumstances are in a person's life, be lavish, excessive, over the top, with gladness as we hand out blessings on others. Do not count the cost or consider what we will get in return. Also, don't give to impress people. Give with a smile in our hearts and impress God. Make Him Smile! Consider Santa Claus who gives in secret and expects nothing in return. He couldn't be happier to release holiday cheer.

Romans 10:13 . . . for, "Everyone who calls on the name of the Lord will be saved."

Dear friends,

There is something so comforting in knowing God is for us, even when we fail Him, disregard Him, and make a mess of everything. However, our life is categorized. In whatever condition we may be, He treats us all equally, and when we cry out for help with a broken heart, He will come and save us. That is what He did when He sent His Son, Jesus. Sometimes children upset dad with their disobedience, but if they humble themselves, and cry out for help, He's there! This I will say, that's the heart of the Father, and He sent His Son. Merry Christmas!

John 15:5 "I am the vine; you are the branches. If you remain in me and I in you, you will bear much fruit; apart from me you can do nothing."

Dear friends,

In our old life, we were worthless, useless, fruitless, and good for nothing . . . Until we choose to give our lives to Christ and abide in Him. Our every intention is selfish and looking out for our own interests. Now that Christ is in our hearts, we may be productive, fruitful, and pleasing to the Father. We are now good for nothing but obedience and giving glory solely to God. It is not about us anymore; it is all about Him. Continue in the grace that has been given us.

Luke 13:3 I tell you, no! But unless you repent, you too will all perish."

Dear friends,

When a hurricane, tornado, earthquake, fire, or any other disaster occurs, the damage is heartbreaking. Life is forever changed and not in a good way. This is when the world seeks help. People start praying and search for some kind of disaster relief. God is loving, kind, merciful, full of compassion and forgiveness. He hears our cries and provides our needs. God is also a shield, fortress, and protector. I like the way Paul writes it, "The Lord will rescue me from every evil attack and will bring me safely to his heavenly kingdom. To him be glory forever and ever. Amen." See, Paul knew his need for God. He knew he could not make it on his own. He knew that he was a sinner in need of a Savior. Therefore, he lived a repentant life. He daily worked out his salvation. He knew he was covered.

Matthew 6:24 "No one can serve two masters. Either you will hate the one and love the other, or you will be devoted to the one and despise the other. You cannot serve both God and money.

Dear friends,

When Jesus saves us, He cleans house. What I mean is that He enters our hearts and gets rid of all the garbage, all the filth, and sends the Holy Spirit to dwell inside of us. But He does not take away our free will. We can choose to either walk in the freedom of His Spirit or crawl back into the sin we were once in and become enslaved all over again. Well, when I gave my heart to Jesus, I meant serious business. For years I walked in that freedom, and it was wonderful. Every day was sweet victory and glorious triumph, as God transformed me from glory to glory. Then I met a person, and I thought this person was wonderful. I gave all my attention to that person's needs and began to spend all my time and energy trying to please someone else. The more I tried to please that person, the more I violated God's word. Slowly, I began to despise God's word. Listen, dear friends; whether it's a friend, lover, boss, official, or any other person, thing, institute, or religion, we need to choose this day whom we will serve. As for me and my house, we will serve the Lord.

Proverbs 3:11 My son, do not despise the Lord's discipline, and do not resent his rebuke, . . .

Dear friends,

A certain father had many sons. He gave the kids a task to do while he went to work. He gave them specific instructions on who was responsible for each task and said, "I want this done by the time I get home." Well, all the kids did their job, except one. That one hated work and despised his father's instructions. He refused to listen and obey. When the father came home, he was forced to discipline this son. This went on all through the boy's youth. Well, that son graduated from Harvard but could never hold a job. He was very smart but always lazy and disobedient. He never wanted to listen to his father's instructions. Everywhere he went, he was thrown out and walked on. My point is this: do not resist the changes God wants to make. They are not always fun, and sometimes they hurt. They involve listening and being obedient, but Daddy knows best.

J

Philemon 1:6 I pray that your partnership with us in the faith may be effective in deepening your understanding of every good thing we share for the sake of Christ.

Dear friends,

How many of us know that we serve a limitless God? There is always more, and we often cry out for more Lord. The problem is that we do not completely understand what we are asking. God knows what it is, but He is usually not going to give it to us until we are ready. How can we be ready for something we do not even know? When something comes that we don't know about it, it is called a surprise. Even good things can become unwelcome surprises when one is unprepared. Paul tells us how to become prepared. Preparation comes through actively communicating and talking about our faith. Fellowship! By sharing we are preparing to grow.

Matthew 19:21 Jesus answered, "If you want to be perfect, go, sell your possessions and give to the poor, and you will have treasure in heaven. Then come, follow me."

Dear friends,

As we welcome another new year, let us make certain that we lack nothing in regard to eternal life. It is very important that we follow Jesus if we want to see eternal life. Remember this, practice God's word if you want to be rich toward God. Quite frankly, if we think we are following Jesus without practicing God's word, we are only fooling ourselves. This I will say, we are not even worthy of being called Jesus's followers if we do not practice God's word. Be a doer of God's word and follow Jesus. Then we will lack nothing.

Made in the USA
Middletown, DE
30 March 2019